The
Music Lover's Guide to the
INSTRUMENTS
of the
ORCHESTRA

The
Music Lover's Guide to the
INSTRUMENTS
of the
ORCHESTRA

MADEAU STEWART

 VAN NOSTRAND REINHOLD COMPANY

NEW YORK   CINCINNATI   TORONTO   LONDON   MELBOURNE

DEDICATED TO
The Hon. Mrs Pamela Jackson
as an encouragement

Printed in Hong Kong

Published in 1980 by Van Nostrand Reinhold Company
A division of Litton Educational Publishing, Inc.
135 West 50th Street, New York, NY 10020, U.S.A.

Van Nostrand Reinhold Limited
1410 Birchmount Road
Scarborough, Ontario M1P 2E7, Canada

16 15 14 13 12 11 10 9 8 7 6 5 4 3 2 1

Library of Congress Cataloging in Publication Data

Stewart, Madeau.
    The music lover's guide to the instruments of the orchestra.

    Bibliography: p.
    Includes index.
    1. Musical instruments.   2. Orchestra.   I. Title.
    ML460.S82   781.9′1   79-13825
    ISBN 0-442-23358-2

Contents

Foreword

Any attempt to enlarge or deepen people's love of music, to furnish them with a closer understanding of the various works to which they listen, has my whole-hearted support. In *The Music Lover's Guide to the Instruments of the Orchestra*, I am convinced that its readers will find precisely what they need: a clear-headed, elegant and often humorous style from which they will learn, and in the learning, enjoy.

There may indeed exist many concert-goers who will remain satisfied simply to be washed over with delicious sound, rather in the manner of a nice warm bath. Far be it from me to be arbitrary or portentous about the value in terms of bliss between ignorance and knowledge. All I can say, as a performing musician, is that I feel that such a book as this will bring a deeper consideration of what we are attempting to convey, perhaps a more sympathetic understanding of the manifold difficulties inherent in these instruments we are forever trying to control so that we may speak through them to our audience and thus narrow the gap between us.

When we speak of the orchestra we should in fact be referring to the entire world family of instruments. This means the conception of a broad agglomerate containing almost every means of music-making. This is an awesome perspective, but a synoptic view is a repository of the collective and collected efforts of mankind to express himself by and with every conceivable kind of sound and noise. There is possibly no effect that a truly imaginative composer cannot achieve by means of the orchestra; there is no style, no idiom, no culture, which cannot be reflected, transmuted, and enabled to speak for itself within the orchestra. It is in recognition of this ineluctible fact that we are encouraged to look back over our shoulders and to delve into the most remote reaches of time.

There is probably no handy material which has not been coaxed into giving out its natural vibration and resonance. Today, we must observe somewhat sourly, plastics and other such man-made fibres have been called into use, in many cases simply as a financial saving. We live in a paradoxical world wherein at the same time communications bring us ever closer to other and to disparate cultures, while the techno-industrialisation of our daily lives is eating away at the very roots that bind us to Nature and to our own individual natures.

This is a perversity which to a great degree music can heal – for it is the Lingua Franca of all human beings, and in whatever form we may listen to it, it is something we can share with each other. It is indeed that great consort: harmony.

> '*From harmony, from heavenly harmony*
> *This universal frame began:*
> *From harmony to harmony*
> *Through all the compass of the notes it ran*
> *The diapason closing full in Man*'

> Milton: *Song for St Cecilia's Day*

Yehudi Menuhin

Preface

'IL NE SUFFIT PAS QUE L'ARTISTE SOIT BIEN
PRÉPARÉ POUR LE PUBLIC, IL FAUT AUSSI QUE
LE PUBLIC LE SOIT À CE QU' ON VA LUI
FAIRE ENTENDRE.'

(*It is not enough that the artist should be
well prepared for the public, the public
must also be well prepared for what it is
going to hear.*)
    – Berlioz

In the whole history of the world's music there never has been any combination of sounds as complex and various as that of the full symphony orchestra. This is what makes orchestral music endlessly attractive and exciting to generations of music lovers, and suggests a book designed to prepare the public for what it is going to hear.

Today it is said that the instruments of the orchestra in their present form have been exploited to their limits; a restless search by composers for new sounds and combinations of sounds has led to the use of electronic devices. Nevertheless, such widely disparate contemporary composers as Elliot Carter and Sir Michael Tippett still find it possible to write for the conventional orchestra. This book is about the instruments of that orchestra, which performs works from the time of Mozart (1756–91) up to the present.

Where technique is concerned, only the most basic information has been offered. For every instrument there are different schools of thought about sound production, fingering, embouchure and so on, some of them diametrically opposed to each other.

In 1873 Rimsky-Korsakov intended to write a book on orchestration that would begin with an exhaustive investigation into the construction and acoustic laws of each instrument. After a year he abandoned this part of the project, not only because it was too ambitious an undertaking, but also because its value to students was questionable. Such an undertaking is also far beyond the scope of this book, and therefore only the barest outline of this aspect of music making has been included.

In spite of much recent research, stimulated by modern interest in the music and instruments of earlier written music, up to the time of Mozart, there remain innumerable mysteries about the origins and development of almost all the instruments of the orchestra. These questions are interesting in themselves, and many are described in this book. Furthermore, the book takes into account the growing desire among musicians and the public to hear early symphonic music (composed since 1750) on the instruments for which it was written, so an attempt has been made to describe what the immediate ancestors of today's instruments look and sound like.

There is no substitute for attending a live concert! This book will have fulfilled its purpose only if it enhances listening pleasure and encourages readers to look into some of the more specialist books listed in the bibliography.

Introduction

The modern symphony orchestra is generally described as having its foundations in the 18th century, at a time when harmonic music was developing. But the roots of the instruments used in the orchestra go much deeper. Many an instrument used in symphonic music was first used in theatre and opera music. As early as the 16th century Gabrieli (1557–1612) and Monteverdi (1567–1643) were masters of a form of instrumentation, often designed to support and blend with voices as well as to produce suitable dramatic or realistic effects. Lully, Rameau, Gluck and Mozart each introduced new instruments into their operatic scores. It is sometimes forgotten that the prehistoric union of singing, dancing and acting to an instrumental accompaniment has absorbed the attention of most composers well into the 19th century. Rossini, Richard Strauss and Wagner were all innovators both in the instruments they scored for and in the way they wrote for them. Purely symphonic orchestration is in fact a comparatively recent art, a climax in its development coming only towards the end of the 19th century, or even in the 20th, with Ravel, Debussy and Stravinsky.

Ensembles, groups or bands of instruments, have existed outside Europe for thousands of years, the ancient court music of Japan – *Gagaku* – and the *Gamelan* or gong music of Bali being two examples. The music of those earliest Eastern ensembles was frequently of a functional nature, designed to accompany particular events, unlike symphonic music, which holds interest by the treatment of good tunes, harmonic progression and above all a kaleidoscope of sounds.

The majority of the instruments of the orchestra originated in the East, and an interesting modern phenomenon is that both the instruments and the music have now returned to the East in their developed form and that the East, Japan in particular, is exporting them all back to Europe and the U.S. Re-issues of many great recordings by pre-war concert artists were available in Japan when they were out of print in the West! Simultaneously there is a vigorous interest in original Eastern music among contemporary composers and audiences: a concert by a Balinese gamelan orchestra was included in the 1979 London series of Promenade Concerts for the first time.

The earliest written music of Europe was mainly functional. Under church and court or private patronage it was composed for particular religious or secular events. But that music was polyphonic, made up of different strands or voices running parallel and interweaving. Clarity of texture was essential to polyphonic music because it was important that the course of each strand or voice could be followed. Although many composers scored their works for specific instruments, some did not, and which instrument played which strand depended not so much on the character of the sound it made as on its compass, or range of notes. If one player (or 'voice') fell ill, a substitute had to be found among the resident resources. So a recorder might take the place of a flute, or a flute the place of some other instrument. This might be called instrumentation.

BELOW
On this painted wooden ceiling at Crathes Castle in Scotland, ladies with Frenchified coiffes play instruments which are not too accurately depicted: a viola da gamba with two sets of f-holes, a flute with a bell and an odd-looking cittern. It was quite respectable for women to play any type of instrument until the 19th century, when only the harp and the piano were considered suitable. This discrimination continued in the 20th century until Sir Henry Wood introduced a woman as leader of the strings, and later Sir John Barbirolli a female timpanist in the Hallé Orchestra of Manchester

ABOVE
The orchestra of the Ueno Academy of Music was photographed in Tokyo in 1905. Japanese interest in Western music was confined to military music until the mid-19th century. The Ueno Academy for the study of the classical repertoire was founded in 1890 and directed by Westerners; its success was short lived. An outstanding feature of this orchestra was that all the violinists were women, in sharp contrast to Western practice of the time

In orchestration, which was developed in symphonic music, each instrument is assigned a specific role in order to produce a specific timbre or colour. Substitution of any sort would produce a distortion of the composer's intentions, once harmony had become more important than polyphony.

The word 'symphony' means simply a harmony of sound. When Chaucer wrote of 'harpe and pype and symphonye' he was referring to the small hand-cranked instrument that today is called the hurdy-gurdy, which can produce more than one note at a time, generally by means of one or two drone strings under a melody string. The use of the word 'symphony' to describe a series of movements of contrasting moods and tempi originated in the practice of stringing together overtures, interludes and postludes from oratorio and opera to make suites, or 'symphonies', which were performed independently. These symphonies were, however, 'mood' music of a sort, indicating to the

audience the general character of the opera or of the next scene. When these movements were divorced from a story, the composer no longer needed to employ conventional sound symbols, such as drums and trumpets for a military scene, to inform the audience about the next scene in the drama. The listener became free to compose his own scenario; it was a new kind of abstract music.

Of course many sound symbols still survive, and are employed to denote a locality, or the weather: harps for heaven and castanets for Spain, oboes and flutes for pastoral scenes with birds, bass rumblings and cymbal clashes for storms with lightning. The list is a fairly long one, and the majority of composers have made use of this international musical shorthand, from Haydn and Beethoven to Mahler and Britten. The sound of the muffled drum is usually a symbol of death.

In every way, Joseph Haydn (1732–1809) is a most important figure in 18th century music. His life span covered many of the major developments in music making, among the most important being the beginning and increase in number of public concerts. It was a period when, though private patronage continued, its domination of the musical scene began to wane. During Haydn's lifetime the piano overtook the harpsichord in popularity, Sebastian Érard improved the harp mechanism, François Tourte perfected the violin bow and the violin itself underwent design changes to give it more volume. Dragonetti, a friend of Haydn, liberated the double bass from its life of subservience, and wind instruments were also being scrutinized with a view to their improvement. In his old age Haydn remarked that he had only just learned how to use the wind instruments, 'and now that I do understand I must leave this world' – as if it were not enough that he was the father of symphonic form and of the string quartet and that a descriptive catalogue of his compositions, which included over a hundred symphonies, would be longer than this book. Haydn was among the first true symphonic orchestrators.

Igor Stravinsky (1882–1971) said, 'It is not, generally, a good sign when the first thing we remark about a work is its instrumentation.' The composers whose work impresses us this way, he said, are not the best composers. Beethoven is seldom praised for his orchestration. But throughout the 19th century the craft of orchestration continued to develop in complexity. Schubert's 'Great' C Major Symphony (1828) is a masterpiece of the art, written by a composer who had little hope of ever hearing the work performed. Antonin Dvořák was a prominent Czech nationalist composer who was hired to come to the U.S. to help inspire American composers to develop their own national tradition; he deeply admired American folk music, but he was also a very homesick Bohemian when he wrote his 'New World' symphony (1893). The result is one of the most popular symphonies ever written. Gustav Mahler was a Bohemian Jew in a Catholic German-speaking country; he was influenced by folk poetry, military band music and much else. All of this is reflected in his extravagant orchestration.

By the end of the 19th century it was the Russians and the French above all who exploited orchestration to such a degree that it was no longer possible not to notice it. Nicolas Rimsky-Korsakov (1844–1908), who was one of Stravinsky's teachers, wrote one of the most important books on the subject of orchestration. He was a Russian naval officer, responsible for the Imperial military bands, as well as a prominent composer in the Russian nationalist school. But perhaps Claude Debussy (1862–1918) was the most unusual colourist of all; often enough it is impossible to identify the instruments that produce the curiously misty perspective of sound in, for example, *Nocturnes* (1900). Debussy was not the first to be influenced by certain characteristics of Eastern music (he had heard the sound of the Balinese gamelan), in which the overtones of a sound are appreciated and cultivated, but he was surely the first to exploit their subtleties so fully.

Voicing

The word *voice* has been important in music from early times well into the present century, but its significance has often been neglected even though it is a key word which, when understood in the context of the history of music, illuminates a crucial difference between the polyphonic and harmonic music.

Throughout the history of music, the human voice has usually been considered to be the most beautiful and perfect of all musical instruments. The ideal sound sought by instrument makers and players was that which most resembled the human, singing voice – even among brass, woodwind and keyboard instruments. The term 'to voice' is even now used by instrument makers and tuners when they make adjustments to refine the sound of an instrument. Some instrumentalists learned to breathe like singers and some string players learned to phrase like singers. But when the great school of polyphonic writing came to an end with the death of J.S. Bach (1685–1750) and harmonic and orchestral music began to develop, that ideal was gradually discarded and every instrument of the orchestra became exploited for its own unique qualities rather than for its ability to imitate. This was a form of liberation which enabled composers to exploit a new range of sounds and effects.

There was however one feature of singing which had not been exploited in instrumental music of the polyphonic era which, when introduced in the 18th century, caused pleased astonishment. This was the vocal practice of crescendo and diminuendo. Formerly instruments had been divided into loud and soft, producing a terraced dynamic range of sound. The harpsichord produces this sort of dynamic range, since some stops are loud and some soft. Echo effects are possible but no variations of volume within a phrase. Articulation was therefore of major importance to polyphonic music and echo effects were used frequently. The swelling of a note or phrase from a whisper to fortissimo introduced a new dimension to 18th century instrumental music; the moulding of a phrase by gradations of volume was a further stage of liberation.

Development of the modern orchestra

The first symphonic orchestras were smaller, playing to smaller audiences in smaller halls, and the instruments themselves were quieter. For a time, more volume was produced by increasing the

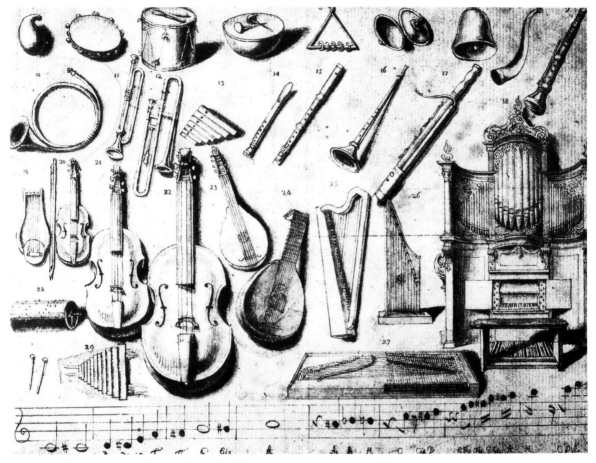

number of instruments. But by the end of the 19th century many of the instruments had been re-designed or modified in some way that not only altered their timbre but added to their volume. Simultaneously pitch rose, adding greater brilliance to the sound. In the 20th century these enlarged forces have been employed indiscriminately to play the music of Rimsky-Korsakov (b.1844), Mozart (b.1756) and Handel (b.1685). And the music was played in larger halls. The result was that the timbre and proportion of sound to the originally conceived texture of the earlier instrumental music was in some considerable measure destroyed. In the opinion of many we were losing touch with the sound of the orchestra as it was conceived by Haydn and Beethoven.

Just as the cycle of the cross-fertilization of cultures has come full circle with the East bringing European music into Europe, so at the same time Europeans are groping towards the past, and performing and recording early symphonic music on the instruments for which it was written. The result could almost be described as the discovery of an entirely new repertoire for the symphony orchestra. People today flock to performances of early music played on early instruments as they once flocked to hear the music of their own time.

The new appreciation of historical accuracy in orchestral playing leads to occasional anomalies on the concert platform. For example, a concert at London's Royal Festival Hall in June 1979 featured the

ABOVE
Daniel Nicolas Chodowiecki (1726–1801) was a Pole who worked in Germany after 1743. Here he has depicted a collection of instruments many of which were already obsolescent at the time. 1. The sack of a bagpipe 2. Tambourine 3. Tenor drum 4. Small kettle drum 5. Triangle with jingles 6. Cymbals 7. Bell 8. Cornett (the holes are in shadow) 9. Hoboy (early oboe) 10. Horn (songle coil) 11. Trumpet 12. Bass trombone 13. Pan pipes 14. Descant recorder 15. Transverse flute with one key 16. Shawm 17. Bassoon 18. Organ 19. Lyre 20. Treble viol and bow 21. Tenor viol 22. Bass viol 23. Cittern 24. Lute 25. Harp 26. Mechanical table harp 27. Clavichord (reversed engraving) 28. Pin barrel from an automated instrument (probably an organ) 29. Xylophone

Academy of St. Martin-in-the-Fields playing symphonies by Mozart and Haydn, the concerto for two violins by J.S. Bach, and Beethoven's First Piano Concerto (in fact the second one he wrote, but the first to be published). The Academy is a chamber orchestra, the right size for early classical music; the Bach concerto was played by an even smaller group, and without the conductor, Neville Marriner. Both the Bach concerto and the Haydn symphony included harpsichord continuo.

The growth of the orchestra

Haydn: Symphony No. 104 ('London') (1795)
  2 flutes, 2 oboes, 2 clarinets, 2 bassoons
  2 horns, 2 trumpets
  2 timpani
  Violins I and II, violas, cellos, basses

Beethoven: Symphony No. 9 ('Choral') (1823)
  1 piccolo, 2 flutes, 2 oboes, 2 clarinets, 2 bassoons
  4 horns, 2 trumpets, 3 trombones
  2 timpani, bass drum, cymbals & triangle
  Violins I and II, violas, cellos and basses
  Chorus and four solo voices

Wagner: *Götterdämmerung* (1872)
  1 piccolo, 3 flutes, 3 oboes, 1 English horn, 3 clarinets, 1 bass
    clarinet, 3 bassoons
  8 horns, 3 trumpets, 1 bass trumpet, 3 trombones, 1 contrabass
    trombone, 2 tenor tubas, 2 bass tubas, 1 contrabass tuba
  4 timpani, cymbals, tenor drum, triangle, bells
  6 harps
  16 first violins, 16 second violins, 12 violas, 12 cellos, 8 basses
  13 solo voices

Ravel: *Daphnis & Chloë* (1911)
  2 piccolos, 2 flutes, 1 alto flute, 2 oboes, 1 English horn, 2 clarinets,
    1 E-flat clarinet, 1 bass clarinet, 3 bassoons, 1 contrabassoon
  4 horns, 4 trumpets, 3 trombones, 1 tuba
  4 timpani, bass drum, cymbals, snare drum, tenor drum, triangle,
    tambourine, castanets, antique cymbals, gong, eoliphone,
    glockenspiel, celesta
  2 harps
  Violins I and II, violas, cellos, basses
  Chorus

An exact number of strings is usually not specified; a Haydn symphony might be played by a Wagnerian string section, but the modern tendency is toward more realistic performance, with perhaps eight first violins and six second violins.
There are many unusual additions in individual modern scores, such as Ravel's eoliphone (a wind machine). Mahler's Seventh Symphony calls for cowbells; Strauss wrote for a thunder machine. Respighi wanted Roman trumpets, while Tippett's Third Symphony includes a flügelhorn. There are also rattles, woodblocks, etc. and one score includes a gramophone record.

In the Beethoven piano concerto, soloist Murray Perahia played the third and least known cadenza which Beethoven wrote for that work, which was full of dynamic variation: loud-soft-loud-soft. Beethoven may have written this cadenza for the very purpose of exploiting that characteristic of the pianoforte, which at that time was still a relatively new instrument. But here is the anomaly: the instrument itself was the usual large Steinway concert grand. For all the soloist's stylishness, the piano sounded boomy, especially in the bass: it would have been far more appropriate for playing Brahms. However, this sort of compromise may continue to be necessary, because the majority of pianists would be unable or unwilling to adapt to the different keyboard technique required by an early piano.

Instrument identification

The characteristic sound of an instrument is determined by the number, strength and duration of harmonics in that sound in relation to the fundamental or actual note played. The technical name for this relationship is *timbre*. Harmonics are sometimes also called overtones, upper partials or, in some cases, sympathetic vibrations. A small, dull thump has fewer and weaker harmonics of shorter duration than has a loud clang from a large bell.

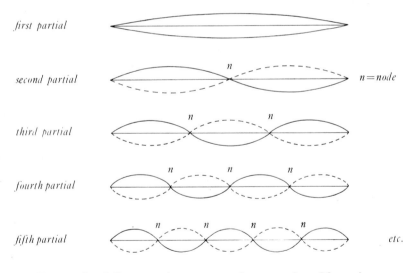

first partial

second partial $n = node$

third partial

fourth partial

fifth partial   *etc.*

LEFT
An unstopped string vibrates its whole length, sounding its fundamental. But it also vibrates at the same time in an infinite number of parts of its length, sounding partials, or harmonics, which become weaker and weaker. These are heard as a complicated set of overtones which give the sound much of its quality. If the string is stopped half-way, then the second partial becomes the fundamental, and so forth. If the vibrating string is lightly touched at any of the nodes, the appropriate harmonic is heard, but with a strange timbre. This might be called for by a composer who wants a very special effect

Harmonics follow a strict pattern of progression. If a string or a column of air is halved, it produces a note an octave higher, but it also always produces a set of harmonics which are exact multiples of the note itself. If the string or the pipe is stopped halfway, or a third, or a quarter or a fifth of the length, and so forth, then one of these harmonics becomes the primary note, but also produces its own harmonics. This is called the harmonic series, and it provides the basis for all the modes and scales there have ever been. The steps between the harmonics are mathematically precise, but of such subtlety that an illustration in conventional notation gives only an approximate position of the harmonics.

Any note played on a musical instrument includes a complex

selection of harmonics of different strength and duration; it is this selection that informs the listener of the identity of the instrument being played. And there is a moment of maximum revelation in the note played: this is the instant of impact of bow, breath or beater on the instrument, because this is the moment when the maximum number of harmonics is present. For instance, the timbre of a large bell is recognized by the richness of the note or fundamental produced by the stroke of the clapper. If that clapper stroke were eliminated and only the reverberation, or series of fading harmonics, were heard, it would be more difficult to identify their source. One reason why it is not always possible to identify an instrument on a recording or during a broadcast is that the initial stroke that has produced the note – the *transient* as it is called – has been attenuated in the course of transmission.

The first harmonic in the series is the octave. Over the centuries much argument and philosophical discussion and experimentation has surrounded the problem of tempering or arranging the harmonic progression or series in a way that would produce a pleasing sequence of notes within that octave. A number of different scales, with varying distances between the notes, were used and this method (called mean tone tuning) seemed perfectly satisfactory until the middle of the 18th century, because there was not a great deal of modulation or changing from key to key in the music. But when composers sought the freedom to modulate from related to unrelated keys, mean tone tuning proved unsatisfactory. The distances between the notes of the scale in the octave and over the whole range of, for example, keyboard instruments were therefore altered again, and the octave was divided into twelve roughly equal steps. This was called equal temperament, and its use was pioneered by J.S. Bach in his 48 Preludes and Fugues, one in every key and each containing daring modulations.

Along with the new freedom to modulate from one key to another, a tendency developed among classical composers to associate the sounds of certain instruments with certain keys. Haydn apparently only ever wrote for the cor anglais (English horn) in the key of E flat major.

Listeners often wonder why one key sounds different from another, and why a composer should bother to write in C major rather than E flat or D. The reason is that it is not possible to arrange the steps of the chromatic scale throughout six to seven octaves or more in equidistant steps; some notes are fractionally sharp, some fractionally flat and unisons between one end of the keyboard and the other are imperfect. Thus some keys could be said to have an 'edgier' quality than others, which have a certain blandness about them. The art of tuning keyboards has now reached such complexity, partly on account of the revival of early music, with its mean tone tuning and different pitches, that there are expensive electronic pitchmeters on sale to assist the tuners.

As equal temperament is a contrived scale, yet each note continues to behave according to the immutable laws of harmonic progression, it can be appreciated that conflicts are produced when the harmonics of that scale clash with those of natural progression. For many, equal

Public concerts first began in America around 1732. The famous Hollywood Bowl in California is an acoustic shell which solves the problem of presenting concerts outdoors

temperament destroyed clarity and sweetness of timbre because of this excitement of alien harmonics. For most instrumentalists and singers it made little difference, since they have no inhibitions about sharpening or flattening a note according to interpretation, and the scales they use defy all the theorists. But it made matters very difficult for the instrument makers, whose skill lay in constructing the body of an instrument so that the right harmonics would be present at the right strength and without buzzing or 'difference tones', as those sometimes painful clashes of harmonics are called. It was in fact partly the adoption of equal temperament that forced instrument makers to re-design and mechanize most of the instruments of the orchestra, thereby appreciably altering their timbre.

The timbre of the whole orchestra depends on the quantity and strength of harmonics in the overall sound. And of course the hall in which the orchestra performs affects its timbre. Some halls, and large churches in particular, respond in too lively a manner, agitating a host of sympathetic vibrations which blur the music. Other halls have what is called a dead acoustic, making impossible the blending of timbres of the different instruments of the orchestra. 'That is why', wrote Berlioz, 'there is no such thing as music in the open air. The most enormous orchestra placed in the middle of an extensive garden open on all sides . . . would produce no effect.'

People who can tell one violin from another or one orchestra from another are relying at least in part on their ability to hear harmonics.

Pitch

The pitch and tuning of the modern orchestra have only been established after long years of argument and research.

To pitch a note means to place it at a particular level, high or low, in the sound spectrum. When two, ten, a hundred or a thousand musicians are to play together, one note of the scale is chosen to determine the relative pitch of all other notes in the scale. That note is middle A on the piano.

Pitch is determined by the number of vibrations per second of a sound wave. The A given out by the oboe or the piano at the start of a concert is 440 cycles per second. This standard and international pitch was only agreed in 1939.

Over the centuries pitch has fluctuated widely from as high as 505.8 cps in 14th century Germany to as low as 373.7 cps in 17th century France. In 1813 Philharmonic pitch was 424 cps, but in 1859 a French commission, which included Berlioz, Rossini and Meyerbeer, proposed 435 cps. By 1874 Philharmonic pitch had risen to 455 cps.

RIGHT
*In a painting by Hans Mielich
(c.1570) Orlando di Lassus
(1532–1594) directs, from a
virginal, a group consisting of viola
da gamba, violin, bassoon, flute,
recorder, trombone, cornett, rackett
and lute. This was the band of the
Munich Court. The lower panel gives
a list of the musicians, the upper a
passage from Ecclesiasticus 32*

There was no uniformity anywhere or at any time and the situation was considered deplorable. It caused embarrassment both to travelling musicians and to instrument makers and, when too high, brought singers to grief on their top notes. Moreover there were often several different pitches in current use: one for the orchestra, one for the home, one for choirs and another for opera. In 1895 strenuous efforts were begun to achieve some sort of uniformity, but it took all of 44 years for international agreement to be reached.

Higher pitch produces greater brilliance but it also attenuates the timbre of an instrument, because the higher a note the fewer the audible harmonics will be present in the sound.

In the 1970s there has been some tendency for pitch to creep up again, but this is counterweighted by the early music revivalists. So now again there may be a number of pitches in current use.

The compasses of the instruments

Each book on instrumentation and each dictionary of music might provide slightly different information on the compasses of the individual instruments; the subject is so complicated that many popular books avoid the subject altogether. There are written ranges, sounding ranges, extended ranges and expressive or working ranges.

The difference between written and sounding ranges applies to transposing instruments. A number of wind instruments fall into this category. For a variety of technical and historical reasons, these instruments are not written for at their true pitch, but produce the effect of that pitch when they are played. This makes things more difficult for people reading scores, and a modernization of the system of notation could probably eliminate it, but it becomes second nature for the musicians themselves, so it doesn't bother them. For example, the working compass of the French horn in F could be written

but it would sound thus

while the extended range might be written

sounding

Extended ranges depend on different factors, not least the ability of the player. In the case of the string instruments, *scordatura*, or alternative tuning of the strings, can raise or lower the compass.

Sometimes the pedal, or lowest, notes on the trombone are not included in tables, because they do not fall in what Rimsky-Korsakov described as the expressive range, as opposed to the range that provides colour or timbre, but is not expressive. To add to the confusion, the lowest note of some instruments has changed over the years; in Beethoven's day the lowest note on the flute was D. Today on the ordinary orchestral flute it is C, although Hindemith, for example, wrote for a flute going down to B. Then there is the celebrated case of the 'basset-clarinet', for which Mozart apparently wrote his popular clarinet concerto: this clarinet could play lower notes than the modern instrument, so that the music had to be edited where the written notes extended too far below the stave. Only in the past few years has the original score been recorded and broadcast by the BBC, so that we could hear what Mozart wrote.

Following the score

There are two principal groups of instruments in the orchestra: resonating and non-resonating. Non-resonating instruments include all the wind instruments because once a player has ceased to blow, the sound also stops. All non-resonating instruments are written on the upper staves of the score, the piccolo or flute coming first and the tuba last. Resonating instruments are those whose sound continues after the player has bowed, plucked or struck the instrument. These include bells, drums and all the stringed instruments including the harp. They are written on the lower staves, the double bass coming last. Voices, if included, are generally written between percussion and strings.

This division of the orchestra into two principal groups reflects, in a way, the history of the development of the orchestra. The massing of bowed strings at the bottom has provided the foundation for all orchestral music ever since small ensembles or chamber orchestras existed. Other instruments were inserted or introduced one by one and piled on top, as it were, the piccolo not being introduced until Beethoven's time.

To be able to read a score is to be able to hear the music on the page. For this a complete musical training is needed. To simply follow a score along with the music is not difficult once instrument identification has been mastered. To follow a score it is well to start by keeping the eyes glued to the stave carrying the music of the first violins, since they are playing most of the time. There are however pitfalls in this method because, in order to economize on space, publishers of miniature scores frequently only print what is being played, and the string staves can suddenly vanish altogether if this section of the orchestra falls silent. The other disconcerting space-saver practised by publishers is to print the music sideways on. If the music is dashing along *prestissimo furioso* the follower can well be lost until the end of the movement.

Before a concert it is as well to go through the score noting the tempo of each movement, any repeats (marked :ll), and printing

The first page of a score: Beethoven's Egmont overture

hazards such as those mentioned above. After a concert it is fun to go through the score a second time, trying to 'hear' the music all over again.

The orchestra on the platform

One of the several possible layouts of the orchestra is illustrated here. Different conductors favour different arrangements, sometimes because of the nature of the work being played and sometimes because of the nature of the hall. But the first violins are invariably placed on the left of the conductor, and the percussion somewhere at the back. Every section of the orchestra has a leader, principal or first desk.

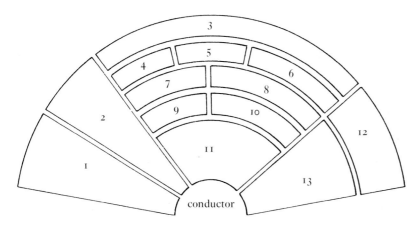

This is one of the many possible arrangements of the sections of an orchestra.
1. First violins 2. Second violins 3. Percussion 4. Horns 5. Trumpets 6. Trombones 7. Clarinets 8. Bassoons 9. Flutes 10. Oboes 11. Violas 12. Double basses 13. Cellos

In Britain, the first violinist is called the leader, from the time up to the end of the 18th century when he literally led the orchestra, before there were conductors. In the U.S. he is called the concert-master. He is always named in concert advertisements and programmes. His duties are onerous for, apart from keeping the first violins together and making sure that they all use the same bowing, he should be able to deputize as conductor if necessary. He should be able to interpret and clarify the wishes of the conductor to the rest of the orchestra (for example, Leopold Stokowski instructed the violins *not* to bow in unison when playing Wagner, in order to achieve a seamless sound in the long lines). The leader will also play any violin solo that occurs in the score. He deserves his round of applause when he walks on to the platform at the start of a concert! Should the leader break a string, the violinist next to him will hand over his instrument and re-string the leader's for him.

The other sections of the strings also have their first desk or leader who, again, will play any solo and make sure there is uniformity of bowing. Leaders of the string sections will be seen to use more exaggerated gestures than those at other desks; this helps to keep players together, and often indicates the emotional mood of the music.

Among wind players there is always a first or principal player. Second desks are expected to turn the pages for the principal and keep a careful count of bars of rest.

In these days of recordings, when performances are note perfect owing to technical surgery on the tapes, many people are denied the exquisite anguish or merriment caused when an instrumentalist blows a raspberry or his instrument in some way lets him down. Pads on wind instruments can stick (cigarette papers are very useful for drying them out), springs can break (elastic bands are handy in this case), screws drop out, reeds split or become saturated and strings can snap. And of course there is the ever-present hazard of someone coming in a beat or a bar too early or too late. One of the reasons for technical surgery on recorded master tapes is that it becomes irritating to hear the same mistake each time the record is played.

'Doubling' is a term frequently used by instrumentalists. This means simply playing two instruments, going from one to the other in the course of the music. A flutist will double on the piccolo, an oboist on the cor anglais. Doubling also refers to two and more instruments playing the same tune, in unison. This is the opposite to *divisi*, when the first or the second violins, or the cellos or basses, divide into two halves, each playing separate parts.

Training of instrumentalists

The oldest music conservatories (so-called because their role was to preserve the science of music from corruption) date from the early 16th century in Italy, but long before that, in the 6th century, there were choir schools in Cathedral cities where the boys, who had to learn reams of church music by heart, were thrashed for singing false. Such choir schools still flourish in major cities, but less memorizing is involved and no thrashing. The emphasis on voice training continued down the centuries, but also included a careful grounding in the theory of music, composition and extemporization. And until the 18th century at least, music was treated as one of the sciences, along with Geometry, Arithmetic and Astronomy (with a particular emphasis on astrology). It is clear from early writings that some sort of relationship was perceived between the harmonious shape and sound of music and that of the Universe, as in Johannes Kepler's book *Harmony of the World* (1619).

Some of the first schooling for instrumentalists seems to have been in the Neapolitan and Venetian Ospedali (hospitals, or charitable institutions), the activities of the latter for girls being described by the Président de Brosses in his *Letters from Italy* of 1739:

They are educated and maintained at the expense of the State, and their sole training is to excel in music. Thus they sing like angels, and play the violin, flute, organ, oboe, violincello and bassoon – in fact there is no instrument so big as to intimidate them. They are cloistered like nuns. They perform without outside help, and at each concert forty girls take part. I swear there is nothing prettier in the world than to see a young and charming nun, in her white frock, with a spray of pomegranate flowers over her ear, conduct the orchestra and give the beat with all the exactness imaginable.

Instruction books for orchestral instrumentalists did not exist until the instruments had emerged from the crisis of their re-designing and mechanization during the 19th century, when symphonic music demanded larger forces and more brilliant technique. To be sure there

The top three staves represent instructions for the musician playing a figured bass accompaniment. The bottom three double staves were originally published by C.P.E. Bach and are his example of how the keyboard improvisation might actually be expressed. See chapter on harpsichord, pp. 116–19

were books of instruction and essays from the 16th century onwards but these were more for the soloists and players in small chamber groups, and ambitious amateurs. *The Modern Music-Master, or the Universal Musician*, by Peter Prelleur, is an example of the last. This was published in 1731 and republished in facsimile in 1964. It begins with 'An Introduction to Singing, after so easy a Method, that Persons of the meanest Capacities may (in a short time) learn to Sing (in Tune) any song that is set to Musick.' And it includes rules for playing a thorough bass and rules for tuning, as well as a brief history of music from the time of the Greeks.

In both Europe and the U.S. the founding of schools, colleges, academies and conservatories corresponded with the establishment of symphonic concerts in the 19th century, although the Paris Conservatoire was founded in 1795 and has always been directed and staffed by the most distinguished of French musicians. All these

RIGHT
A promenade concert at Covent Garden before it burned down in 1858. Orchestra, massed bands, choir, organ, piano and solo singer are conducted by Louis Jullien; behind him is the velvet-covered chair into which he would sink, exhausted, after particularly strenuous work. This picture is by Alfred Concanen (1835–1886), one of the most famous designers of covers for Victorian sheet music

establishments have their own orchestras, thus providing students with a grounding in the classical repertoire. And today quite young people achieve remarkable ability in the many youth orchestras and bands that exist. Singing, harmony, counterpoint, composition, aural training, history and appreciation are all part of the contemporary curricula; more recently instruction on the performance of early music has gradually (if somewhat grudgingly) been introduced. Moreover, since the beginning of the century books of orchestral studies have been produced for all the different instruments, as well as innumerable manuals of instruction. There is, for example, a set of orchestral studies for each and every instrument devoted exclusively to the works of Richard Strauss.

It has been sourly remarked that orchestral players are failed soloists, but this is unjust. The life of the orchestral player is arduous and requires a particular spirit of devotion, as well as the ability to get on with a large body of colleagues. Daily rehearsals and performances, long journeys, foreign tours, awkward halls with poor facilities, awkward conductors as well as awkward soloists all contribute to what, without that devotion, would constitute an intolerable strain. Moments of personal glory are mostly few and brief, but in compensation there is the exhilaration of being swaddled in the warmth of the music – a fact that seems to contribute in some measure to the longevity of orchestral instrumentalists in general as well as conductors in particular.

The rise of the conductor

The history of conducting is rich in dramatic, spiteful, hilarious and gossipy tales from at least the time of Lully (1632–1687) onwards. Lully is celebrated for having struck his foot instead of the floor when beating time, causing an injury that led to gangrene and to his death. The baton can be a lethal instrument in more senses than one. In his *Memoirs* Berlioz recounts how at a critical moment during the performance of his *Requiem* the conductor Habeneck, who was probably involved in some anti-Berlioz feud, calmly put down his baton and took a pinch of snuff. Berlioz, being present and vigilant, sprang forward waving his arms and saved the situation. Smashing and hurling of batons are not unknown in moments of keen stress; in the author's experience furniture was once used as a weapon of protest during a rehearsal.

Until roughly the middle of the 19th century conducting or directing was the composer's job. Some music was hastily written and copied, sometimes only in bare outline, the score itself in a form of shorthand. Thus only the composer knew all the details of the music. He was greatly assisted by the fact that the instrumentalists were thoroughly trained in the grammar or theory of music. The composer could assume that they would be capable of interpreting the outlines in the appropriate manner, extemporizing if necessary. It was towards the end of the 19th century that the conductor was established as a soloist in his own right, although well before that Louis Jullien (1812–60) had already practised some of the more megalomaniac characteristics of later conductors, notably by conducting Beethoven

COVENT GARDEN QUADRILLE.

COMPOSED EXPRESSLY FOR & PERFORMED WITH THE GREATEST SUCCESS AT THE
PROMENADE CONCERTS, COVENT GARDEN THEATRE,
CHARLES COOTE JUNR.

wearing white kid gloves and with a jewelled baton handed to him on a silver salver. Jullien also gave *Concerts Monstres* in Britain with 400 instrumentalists plus three choruses and three military bands. Several times bankrupt on account of his exuberantly lavish performances, not surprisingly Jullien died in a Parisian lunatic asylum.

Various methods of directing or conducting were used in early times for different combinations of instrumentalists and singers. The most disturbing was practised by those called 'wood choppers'; these used a heavy stick which cracked down on the music desk or floor in a series of explosions that must have drowned out some of the music. Vigorous foot stamping had much the same effect. Bare hands, rolled up music and wands were also used. Both Bach and Haydn directed their music from the organ when occasion demanded, and in his early years Beethoven directed from the harpsichord. Double conducting was also common. For this the conductor directed from the keyboard while at the same time the principal violinist, who might have rehearsed the orchestra, flourished his bow to mark the time and the mood. This is the historical basis for the role of today's 'leader' of the orchestra.

For a time during this century the idea prevailed that instrumental works of earlier centuries received incompetent and slapdash perform-ances, which were in no way to be compared to those produced by modern virtuoso conductors such as Toscanini (both feared and revered), Sir Thomas Beecham (also famous as a raconteur of hilarious stories against other conductors) and Furtwängler (whose curiously serpentine and indecisive beat gave the instrumentalists the jitters but could produce marvellous effects). But those conductors inspired different rather than superior performances. The early symphonists would not, after all, have written as they did, nor striven to evolve techniques of composition demanding greater technical ability from the instrumentalists, had performances of their works been charac-terized by out-of-tune playing and frayed ensemble.

The majority of composer-conductors such as Bach and Mozart were meticulous in the preparation of their works, and Gluck (1714–87) in particular is renowned for his exhaustive and exhausting attention to every minute detail in the score. He was, it is said, more fearsome than Toscanini, and such was his severity that when rehearsed by him the musicians demanded and received double pay. It was not uncommon for not only each section but also individual instrumentalists to be strictly drilled in their parts, nor for the composer, conductor or director to go round helping individuals to tune, as well as snatching up an instrument here and there to demonstrate his intentions.

Much instruction and guidance has always been conveyed by singing – if, in many cases, that is the right way to describe the curious repertoire of noises that some conductors make. One of the most remarkable unofficial recordings ever made must be of Toscanini rehearsing the orchestral part of an opera, and singing the whole of the coloratura part himself. Toscanini was famous for his vocalizing, but during concerts and recordings it was manifestly involuntary.

The emergence of the solo conductor was not solely due to a

change in the style of the music, the gradual disappearance of the keyboard as a guiding instrument, nor to any particular musician who practised a new fashion. It was a combination of all these plus developments in music printing and publishing.

The progress of the development of music printing took place over the centuries in various countries, and involved a number of different processes leading from crude woodcuts to increasingly accurate and detailed scores and parts. This in its turn encouraged and enabled composers to write out their music in greater and more expressive detail. Once ornamentation and cadenzas were written out, phrasing and types of bowing indicated as well as dynamics and tempo (sometimes by metronome marks), then the composer had in a sense written himself out of part of his job. Moreover since the instrumentalists were presented with almost fully expressed parts to play from, they no longer needed to be as thoroughly grounded in the grammar of music. Extemporization, which was as much of a display of musicianship as of technical fluency, could now wither away. Anyone with a printed score and a group of proficient instrumentalists could mount performances without having to consult the composer.

By the end of the 19th century cheap printing encouraged the publication of immeasurable quantities of inferior music, as well as new editions of the classics. In these new editions the skill of the printers was exploited to 'express' the music in a manner that was most agreeable to the musicians and audiences of the time. This contributed to a mounting misunderstanding of the true nature of the earlier music. For example, the keyboard works of Bach were reproduced with diminuendo and crescendo marks, and additional slurring quite apart from a liberal strewing of pedal marks, a feature undreamed of at that time.

Nevertheless, during the rise of the solo conductor and the publication of fully expressed scores, all major composers continued to conduct or direct their own works. Beethoven in his later years was embarassingly hindered by his deafness. Schumann was inclined to forget what he was doing. Mendelssohn was held in high esteem because he devotedly conducted both old music and new works of other composers. Weber was the first of the true modern conductors of opera. Berlioz, who wrote about the theory of the art of conducting (as indeed did Wagner), was always complaining about the crimes of other conductors. Verdi was called 'he of the one hundred rehearsals.' Liszt wanted to make the conductor 'seemingly superfluous' and Richard Strauss, after an over-energetic start, decided that 'conducting can be done quietly.' Stravinsky, a model of restraint, thought that conductors betrayed the music by personal and arbitrary interpretation adding that 'la musique doit être transmise et non interprétée' (music should be transmitted, not interpreted).

Among the non-composers who gave impetus to the new role of the solo conductor were Habeneck (1781–1849) and Hans von Bülow (1830–1894). Habeneck, eager to introduce new classics to his audiences, was a great rehearser (his performance of Beethoven's Ninth Symphony was preceded by three years of preparation and rehearsal) but he nonetheless set the precedent of tampering with scores. Hans von

Bülow, who conducted the first performance of Wagner's *Tristan and Isolde*, made a habit of conducting from memory and is credited with having encouraged the exercise of personal display – although Jullien must surely have preceded him in this matter.

In spite of the excellence of printing in the late 19th century many of the great composers, Mahler and Rimsky-Korsakov among others, followed Habeneck's example and tampered with the works of their earlier masters, both re-orchestrating and altering the music of, for example, Gluck, Weber and even Beethoven. In this century Stokowski will be remembered for his inflated orchestrations of many keyboard works of Bach, but this popularization was no worse than those monolithic versions of Handel's *Messiah* so beloved of Sir Malcolm Sargent and others. None of these forms of distortion will survive much longer, because printers and publishers have given a new impetus to the art and understanding of musical performances by reproducing not only *urtexts* or original texts approved by the composer, but an increasing number of facsimile reproductions of scores (Handel's conducting score of *Messiah* is an example), so that the new wave of music directors, ardently dedicated to authenticity, can restore the symphonies of Haydn and Mozart and the choral works of Bach to their proper proportions.

The conductor's role today

As the orchestra expanded and scores became more complicated, firm direction of the instrumentalists became increasingly necessary. Berlioz recounts how 'in a festival where 1200 performers were assembled under my direction' he used four chorus masters and two sub-conductors to 'establish the most perfect unity ever witnessed.'

Unity of intonation, phrasing, tempi and volume as well as internal balance are controlled by the conductor who, according to Sir Adrian Boult, should be master of four or five orchestral instruments, have played for years in an orchestra, know the whole classical repertoire and have, among other things, a constitution of iron.

Stick technique, or beating time, varies with the conductor. Clarity is very important. On the whole the older and wiser the conductor, the more restrained his gestures. Showmen who conduct with dramatic gestures, now sagging at the knees, now appearing to try to reach some object on a top shelf, may impress the audience but are not likely to impress members of the orchestra. If a concert is well prepared in rehearsal by the conductor, the musicians will know their part, respond as rehearsed, give of their best, and would prefer the conductor to address them rather than the audience.

Rehearsals can be as interesting as concerts, for to be present when the conductor is dissecting a work and then moulding it to his own conception not only deepens understanding of the music but often reveals passages which contain technical difficulties. Some conductors may rehearse sections of the orchestra separately, some run through a work and then pick up on ragged or unsatisfactory sections. Others will begin with what they consider difficult passages, and then play through the whole work. Throughout a score the bars are numbered or lettered and so are all the separate parts of the instrumentalists; instead

of saying 'Go back to the oboe solo' the conductor simply gives a letter or a figure. If in the course of a concert someone loses his place, someone else will somehow convey one of these signs to him.

All players are supposed to try to keep their eye on the conductor, watching his stick. But they also have to watch their parts. Sir Adrian has been one of the non-demonstrative school of conductors, pointing out that he always keeps his wrist at a level just above his waist, so that the player always knows where to look when he flicks his eyes up from the score. On the other hand, Furtwängler's was a highly Romantic, almost improvisory style, so that the players could never be quite sure what he was going to do: when this method worked, as in his 1954 recording of Schumann's Fourth Symphony, the results were magical; when it didn't work the result could be disaster, as in a recorded broadcast of Beethoven's Fifth Symphony, when the clarinet started playing before the rest of the orchestra.

Orchestral musicians are a special breed: merciless if there is any sign of incompetence or indecision, they are as warm woolly lambs for conductors they respect. To his long list of qualifications Sir Adrian added that a conductor should 'be ready to appear good-humoured in the face of the most maddening frustrations.'

Sir Adrian was never one of those who inspired rancour among musicians, but this section would be incomplete without an example of the spiteful sort of anti-conductor story which musicians greatly enjoy. A letter to *The Times* of London in the 1950s ran as follows:

Dear Sir,

On September 1 the BBC Symphony Orchestra, conducted by Sir Malcolm Sargent, played the Overture to *Figaro*, by Mozart, in 2 min. 59 sec. Is this a record?

I am, sir, your obedient servant,

D.M. Rendell
London

THE
WOODWIND
INSTRUMENTS

The *Flute*

compass of the flute

The part for the flute is written on the top stave of a full score, even when the higher sounding instrument, the piccolo or 'little' flute, is used. The compass of the flute is three octaves from middle C, but a good player can obtain a few notes above this. The piccolo sounds an octave above, but from D.

The flute is the only woodwind instrument held crosswise, parallel to the shoulders. Sometimes it is made of dark wood, sometimes of glittering silver. The sound, which is produced by blowing across the embouchure or blow hole, has a relatively simple and uncoloured quality due to the small number of harmonics present in it. When the breath strikes the sharp edge of the embouchure it enters the tube, sets the column of air in motion and this in its turn agitates the body of the instrument.

compass of the piccolo (sounds an octave higher)

The three sections of the flute fit together by means of slides. The head joint is slightly tapered towards the stopped end, but the other two joints are cylindrical. The inner surface of the tube is perfectly smooth and shiny so that the vibrating column of air can flow over it unimpeded. The sixteen keys are padded with felt covered by animal skin or some synthetic; these close the holes hermetically at the lightest touch. The keys, which are worked by small steel springs, all stand open when the flute is not in use or when the only open note (C sharp)

RIGHT
A flautist of the Moscow State Orchestra

FAR RIGHT
A selection of transverse instruments. Left to right: a modern piccolo, an Astor boxwood and ivory flute, a modern silver flute, and an ivory and silver flute by Louis Drouet

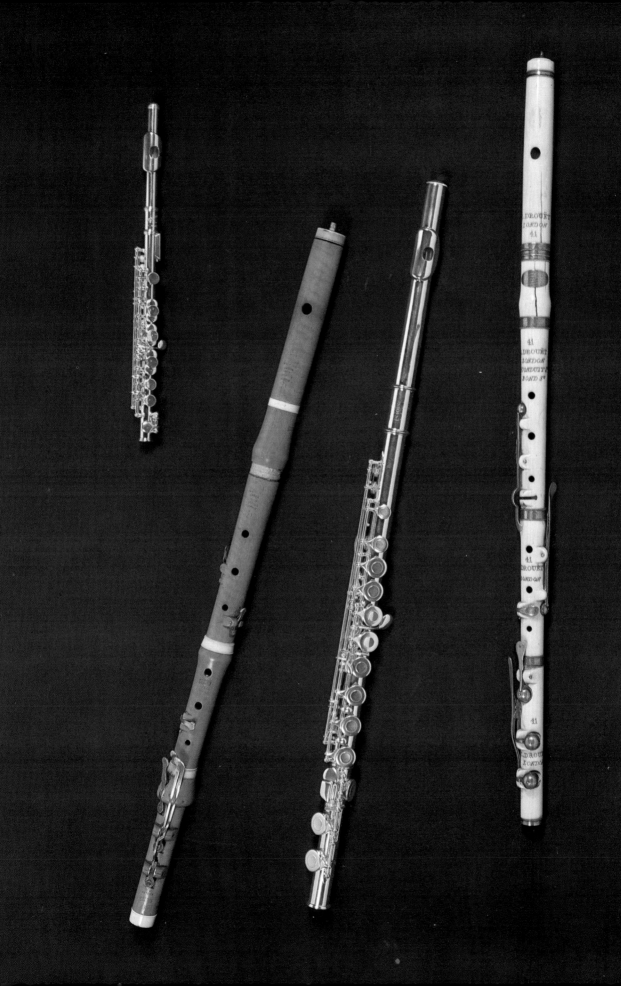

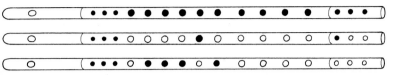

bottom C

middle C

top C

is being played. Bottom C is produced by closing all the keys. From the first to the third octave an increasingly complex system of cross- or fork-fingering is needed to obtain all the chromatic notes of the scale. This is a method of using different combinations of open and closed holes in order to divide the column of air into the appropriate lengths to produce the different notes.

The choice of material for a flute is a matter of personal taste, some favouring the richer, mellower timbre of wood, others the more sparkly quality produced by silver. The former warms up slowly and maintains its temperature (and therefore its pitch) fairly well; the latter goes hot and cold quickly. Only the most affluent flute player can afford one made of gold, a soft and easily excited metal, and its rich glow is unlikely to be seen in an orchestra. Piccolos are also made of wood or metal and they have the same system of fingering.

History

The word flute has been given such a variety of different derivations that its true etymology remains a mystery. Sir John Hawkins, who wrote the celebrated *General History of the Science and Practice of Music*, published in 1853, and republished in facsimile in the U.S. in 1963, provides the following charming but questionable illumination: 'The word flute is derived from *fluta*, the Latin for Lamprey or small eel taken in the Sicilian seas, having seven holes, the precise number of those in front of the flute, on each side, immediately below the gills.'

The first flutes did have but seven holes or less, but they didn't have gills. Anyway, their cradle is unlikely to have been Sicily. The history of the transverse or cross flute is wonderfully confused by the wild enthusiasm of flute historians themselves, who have named every blown tube whether it be held vertically, diagonally, and with or without reed, by the sacred name of flute. Even the recorder has been confused with the flute. Two thousand and more years BC the Chinese played the transverse flute, and still do in the traditional music that survives there. But that stray fact leads nowhere. Existence of the flute in early Greek and Roman times is skimpy and confused by scholars who translated *tibia* and *aulos* – both vertically held reed pipes – as flute. It is only from the late 12th century onwards that there is definite proof that the transverse flute existed in Europe. It is illustrated in a work by the Abbess of Hohenburg called *Hortus Deliciarum* and is labelled a tibia.

For the fullest description of the early flute and all the other instruments of the period, *Harmonie Universelle*, published in Paris in 1636–7 by Father Marin Mersenne, is the most important book; reference is regularly made to Mersenne by scholars burrowing into the past for information about ancestral music and musical instruments.

ABOVE
The flute has sixteen holes and keys. In some instances one key operates two to three keys. The drawing shows how the air in the tube is broken up by open and closed keys for bottom C, middle C and top C

FAR LEFT
Left to right: oboe, oboe d'amore and cor anglais (English horn)

35

RIGHT
Two pipes pictured on a wall painting in a columbarium (a subterranean sepulchre) on the Appian Way, begun in 312 BC. On the left pipe a broad reed is used; the player covers the holes with the second joint of the fingers rather than the tip. This method is still used by performers in a direct line to the ancient tradition, such as that used by shepherds

From the 17th century onwards the flute gained increasing importance in music and began to attract the attention of innovators. A landmark in its history was the publication in about 1699 of the first book of instruction: *Principes de la Flute Traversière ou Flute d'Allemagne*, by the instrument maker Jacques Martin Hotteterre. By now the flute had acquired one key, for the little finger. And such is the mounting interest in early music and instruments in this century that the work was translated and republished in the U.S. in 1968.

The republication of the *Principes* was preceded by one of even greater importance, which was *On Playing the Flute*, by the flute tutor to Frederick the Great, Joachim Quantz (1697–1773). First published in 1752, this is a veritable mine of information about all aspects of music making of the period. The flute by then had a quite considerable repertoire, mainly French, to which Quantz and Frederick together added hundreds more concerti. Frederick played an ivory instrument of conical bore with two keys, and primitive though this may seem it is clear from the Quantz concerti that the instrument was already extremely agile. Flautists who have played these early flutes have found that, although their volume is smaller, their timbre has a sweetness that the modern flute has lost. In other words early flutes are not inferior to modern ones, but simply different; and whether made of ivory or boxwood, with beautifully turned joints, they were certainly more elegant. It is not surprising that they now fetch substantial sums in auction rooms.

The highly mechanized flute we know today was developed by Theobald Boehm (1793–1881). By this time, with the increase in the size of the orchestra and concert halls, a more powerful sound was needed, as well as a wider compass and greater agility. Moreover, equal temperament, in which the octave was divided into steps of almost equal spacing, had been adopted, and the old system of boring the holes according to mean tone tuning (a fact that has led some people to declare that early flutes were out of tune) had to be abandoned.

Boehm, an apprenticed goldsmith as well as a flautist, eventually came to study the physics of music. This enabled him to redesign the flute completely. Jean Hotteterre, grandfather of the author of *Principes*, had introduced the conical bore; Boehm returned to the cylindrical with a parabolic head joint. He also changed and enlarged the positions of all the finger holes and the embouchure and added the complicated keywork mounted on rods along the body of the instrument. His model of 1847 was awarded a gold medal in the Great Exhibition of 1851 in London because 'all the notes are equally fine.' Before he died Boehm wrote that 'alterations can be made ad infinitum, but nothing yet has been better than my system, which will very likely remain the best.' This proved to be the case: all flautists today play flutes and piccolos of the Boehm system. (An ambitious Mr Mathews, who constructed a flute with 28 keys of silver mounted on a tube of gold, with an ivory head joint and square embouchure, was not heard of again.)

Technique

A flute player does not simply breathe into his flute. The beginning of every musical phrase is articulated by pronouncing the letter T. In staccato passages every note is attacked with a T, and in rapid staccato the letters T-K are pronounced. In very fast or triple tonguing this becomes T-K-T T-K-T. A special effect can be produced by rolling an R in the English fashion, with the tongue behind the teeth; this is called flutter tonguing.

The muscles round the mouth and in the cheeks are much exercised when playing the flute and an off-duty flautist can sometimes be identified by the permanent and somewhat enigmatic grin on his face. In the lower register the muscles are slack and the stream of air across the embouchure broad and slow. In the upper registers the stream of air becomes narrower and accelerated and the muscles have to be tautened. The cavities in the head are forms of resonating chambers, and a good flautist will know how to make use of these, like a singer, to give more volume and character to the timbre he is producing. The same technique is used for the piccolo, but on account of its high register, which involves constant exercise of taut muscles, flute players do not like playing both instruments. The muscles used in the lower register lose their flexibility after a great deal of playing in the upper register.

As with all wind instruments good breath control is all-important. The diaphragm must be well-supported and therefore a good upright position always maintained. A flautist who slumps and lets his instrument sag in a diagonal direction will probably produce a weak and puffy tone. Any tone that is in the slightest breathy is to be deplored, and is a true waste of breath, but it is a fact that playing in an orchestra can damage good tone production. Surrounded by a large number of other instrumentalists who singly or in groups produce

more volume, and with relatively brief moments to be heard as a soloist, opportunities to keep the ear alert to and maintain beautiful tone are infrequent. And without good, clear tone throughout all three registers, particularly the top one which inclines to sound screamy, the flute is nothing more than an instrument of great agility and shallow musical interest.

Repertoire

According to Berlioz the flute 'is an instrument well-nigh devoid of expression, but which may be introduced anywhere and everywhere, on account of its facility in executing groups of rapid notes, and in sustaining high sounds useful in the orchestra for adding fullness to the upper harmonies.' This is a fair description of the way the flute is generally written for in orchestral works, but there are many exceptions. The sounds of the middle and upper registers combine well with any ensemble and add lustre. The lower register lacks penetration but has a soft and seductive quality. 'These low sounds', wrote Berlioz in his *Treatise on Instrumentation*, 'are seldom, or else ill, employed by the majority of composers.' All the great orchestrators have however always known how to write for the low register.

Overtures, whose function is, after all, to arrest the attention and raise the level of expectancy, are happy hunting grounds for instrumental passages of particular interest and excitement. One that makes most flautists tremble with terror occurs in the Andantino of Rossini's *William Tell* overture. This florid passage of rapid upward and downward leaps is set against a languorous Swiss-type melody played on the cor anglais. Beethoven, in the overture *Leonora No. 3*, uses the low register in a passage of surprising boldness which starts from low D and rapidly clambers upward to declare the main theme, followed by downward splashes from the high register; this is a prominent and important passage in the overture. Equally prominent and important is a long and mostly low-register passage in Mendelssohn's overture *A Midsummer Night's Dream*. On account of its length and absence of moments for snatching a breath this is somewhat dreaded by flautists; moreover, conductors fail to scale down the volume of the supporting orchestra sufficiently, so the solo is not clearly heard – but the advantage of this is that the flautist is able to leave out a note here and there in order to take a breath.

The ethereal lamenting of the flute in Gluck's 'Dance of the Blessed Spirits' in *Orpheus and Euridice* is in striking contrast to its erotic quiverings in Debussy's *Prélude à l'Après-midi d'un Faune*, which starts on the weakest note of the instrument, C sharp.

To many composers flute timbre has a bird-like quality. Beethoven used it to imitate the nightingale in his 'Pastoral' Symphony, and numerous other composers have given it twittering roles. At the end of the 19th century, when the popularity of the flute was at its zenith, many pieces for voice and chirruping flute were popular, among them Bishop's 'Lo, here the gentle lark.' One little-known 20th century work of great energy and sensitivity is *Lie Strewn the White Flocks*, a Pastoral by Arthur Bliss for chorus, drums, string orchestra, solo flute and piccolo and mezzo-soprano. In this 'The Pigeon Song' is among the loveliest pieces ever written for voice and flute.

There is an old joke which asks 'What is more dreadful than a concerto for flute?' The reply is 'A concerto for two flutes.' Certainly no flute concerto, be it by Vivaldi, Mozart or Ibert, is much more than charming and elegant. Probably the most serious and best-known work for flute and chamber orchestra is the Suite in B Minor by J.S. Bach, but the last movement, a Badinerie, is often taken at a cracking pace for the sake of showing off brilliant technique in a difficult piece – which it isn't.

Since the lower register of the flute is little used because of its lack of penetration, the alto flute, whose compass lies a fourth lower, is very rarely used and then only by composers such as Rimsky-Korsakov and Ravel, at a time when orchestration had nearly become an art in its own right. The shriek of the piccolo, on the other hand, can be heard over the loudest passages played by the largest orchestra. The lower register of the piccolo is feeble and uninteresting, but its upper registers have a jaunty vulgarity that has been used for brief solos by Tchaikovsky (himself a flautist), Bartók in his *Concerto for Orchestra* and by Britten in his *Young Person's Guide to the Orchestra*. A quantity of trivial pieces for piccolo and band were written at the end of the last century, but these are best described as music hall turns, for they depend on brilliant execution for any effect they might make. The piccolo has remained an instrument most suitable for strengthening the higher register of the full orchestra and for the imitation of shrieking winds, banshees and other wild and diabolical forces.

Flute repertoire

Rossini: Overture, *William Tell*
Beethoven: Overture, *Leonora No. 3*
Mendelssohn: Overture, *Midsummer Night's Dream*
Gluck: 'Dance of the Blessed Spirits' from *Orpheus and Euridice*
Debussy: *Prélude à l'Après-midi d'un Faune*
Beethoven: Symphony No. 6 ('Pastoral')
Bishop: 'Lo, here the gentle lark'
Bliss: 'The Pigeon Song' from *Lie Strewn the White Flocks*
Bach: Suite in B minor
Bartók: *Concerto for Orchestra*
Britten: *Young Person's Guide to the Orchestra*

One of the most famous of all flute parts is the opening of Debussy's   *L'Après-midi d'un Faune*

The The
Oboe & Cor Anglais

compass of the oboe

In a full score the part for the oboe is written on the second stave from the top, under that of the flute. The compass is two octaves and a sixth, from B flat, a whole tone below middle C on the piano.

The timbre of the oboe can be identified more easily and quickly than that of any other instrument of the orchestra because during tuning up it can be heard sounding long, steady As to which the whole orchestra, in what seems like a total chaos of sound, tune their strings, pipes and percussion.

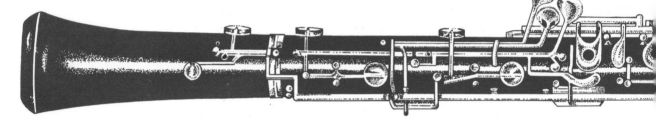

compass of the cor anglais

Made of grenadilla, rose or cocus wood, the oboe has a narrow conical bore terminating in a slight flare or bell. It is held vertically and the double reed, which is mounted in the top, is held in the player's mouth. When blown the lips of the double reed start beating; this drives beaten air into the pipe which then becomes alive with sound. The quality of sound or timbre depends to a major degree on the dimensions of the reed, the grain and its density.

Like the flute, the oboe can be dismantled into three sections and carried discreetly in a small case along with what looks like a small flue brush, used to dry out condensation in the bore at the end of a performance. The precious reeds will very likely be nursed in a small box which allows them adequate ventilation when they are not in use.

The oboe has an elaborate system of keys but, unlike the flute, there is more than one system. The choice of system, as of reed, is a personal matter which is often determined by the nationality of the player or of his teacher.

History

The name oboe derives from the French *haut bois*, meaning literally high wood, but in musical terms, loud instrument. This in its turn derives from early times when instruments were classed as loud or soft, the recorder for example often being called *flûte douce*.

'Who would suspect,' wrote David Munrow in his book *Instruments of the Middle Ages and Renaissance*, 'listening to the intimate and seductive tone of the orchestral oboe today, that it was the offspring of . . . an aggressive outdoor parent.' And still today that aggressive, reedy sound, alive with strong upper partials or harmonics, can be heard outdoors in four continents of the world, playing mostly for secular merry-makings, but also for weddings and religious ceremonies.

The double reed pipe has been known for many centuries. The *aulos* of ancient Greece is the most obvious example, but a pair were found in the royal cemetery at Ur, the city of the moon god of ancient Sumer, dated at approximately 2800 BC; their sophistication indicates that the instrument was known a good time before this. It will never be known whether the cradle of the double reed pipe was in the Sumerian world or whether it was developed in different countries at different times. Europe is said to have received it from the East sometime in the 12th century – or a form of it, called the shawm. This was made from one block of wood with a pronounced flare at the bell. At the base of the staple carrying the reed there was a metal disk or pirouette which

LEFT
A musician preparing to play bulbed pipes, from an Etrurian vase in the British Museum. There is a theory that the reeds were inserted into the bulbs, the lowest bulb providing the shortest length of tube and the top the longest. This would have allowed the player to play in two different modes without altering the fingering

ABOVE
The oboists of the Chicago Symphony Orchestra

was pressed firmly against the mouth of the player. When the player blew, his cheeks distended and became a form of air reservoir. In ancient civilizations, as well as more recent folk cultures, the players would bind their cheeks with material when playing. This served two purposes: it concealed the disfigurement caused by distension, and also assisted control. These players also used what has been called the circular form of breathing, which is used by glass blowers: the pressure on the cheeks enables the player to blow out through his mouth while simultaneously breathing in through his nose.

From the reign of Edward III (1327–1377) in England bands of oboe players called wayghtes, or waits, were employed to mark the merry seasons as well as to attend on Magistrates and Officers the 'pomps and ceremonies'. A wait was thus often another name for an oboist or the instrument itself. But shawm, derived from calamus, a Latin word meaning reed, was its proper name.

The first indoor or domesticated oboes were developed in France and by the mid-17th century were introduced into opera scores. By now the flare of the bell had been reduced and the outstanding pirouette abandoned: the staple carrying the reed stood clear of the rim of the pipe itself. The sound lost its rural roughness and became sweet and tame. From the end of the 18th century onwards an increasing number of keys were added, the characteristic bulge beneath the vestigial pirouette was slimmed away, boxwood was abandoned as a material and a fully chromatic oboe, described as 'the most elaborate

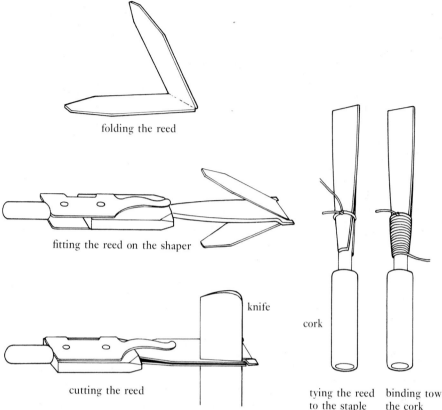

folding the reed

fitting the reed on the shaper

knife

cutting the reed

cork

tying the reed
to the staple

binding toward
the cork

and complicated of reed instruments' was developed, mainly by the Parisian maker Frederic Triébert, who virtually re-designed the instrument in the mid-19th century. Triébert of the 19th century was to the oboe what Hotteterre was to the 17th century flute; instruments of either of these makers, along with those by the English Stanesby and the French Cahusac, both of the 18th century, are now collector's pieces only to be marvelled at in museums or private collections.

Technique

The oboist will often be seen sucking at the reed as though it were a lollipop; this is to moisten it, retaining its flexibility. This habit might have provided the origin of the expression 'to wet one's whistle'; if the reed were too dry or too sodden, squawks and squeaks would reward the player.

As oboists use hard or soft reeds according to their preference as well as the nature of the music, and different makes of instruments have different bores and fingering, the basic playing techniques also vary. So does the timbre and the degree of vibrato exercised. The question of how much, if any, vibrato should be used in playing the oboe has been hotly debated but, like all musical matters where a question of taste is involved, no firm conclusion can be reached. No amount of evidence in its favour on historical grounds, or that it can give greater projection to the sound, can convince some people that it is not inelegant or, in the case of late 18th and early 19th century

ABOVE
The oboe is an instrument with a personality of its own. No two players will get exactly the same tone, and every serious player makes his or her own reeds, for two related reasons: to get the desired tone and to avoid depending on commercially made reeds. These drawings describe the process, but most oboe players will be glad to talk about it at length!

music, unauthentic; while others find an unwavering sound boring.

In spite of having the reed in the mouth, the oboist can pronounce spirited strings of double and triple tonguing, as well as flutter tonguing. A combination of dexterous finger work and embouchure control can produce glissandi. A muted sound can be produced by stuffing a handkerchief up the bell. Curiously enough the dynamic range of the oboe creates a problem because the bore is narrow, and to be effective it has to be finely controlled. Little lung power is needed to play it and fortissimo is not produced by simply blasting additional hot air into the reed. Piano to forte is produced by maintaining steady breath control, increasing air pressure and adjusting the reed in the mouth in a manner that allows it to vibrate freely without going out of tune. Many oboists lovingly make their own reeds – a process involving a number of sharpcutting tools and gouges – and will discuss the 'scrape' with anyone interested enough to listen to a description of this critical art.

A good reed and a good embouchure are complementary and produce good tone. But such are the vagaries of fashion or of habit that whatever the tone or timbre produced by the oboist in an exposed solo passage, there is sure to be someone in the audience who has heard something different and preferable.

Repertoire

Some say that Lully first scored for the oboe in his *Ballet de l'Amour Malade* in 1657, some say it was Cambert in his opera *Pomone* in 1671. Whatever the truth, it was not until the 18th century that the oboe achieved any importance in orchestral music. But there is something rather curious and touching about at least a part of its repertoire for, once this wild instrument of the open air had been tamed and domesticated, a large number of composers, from Handel in *Messiah* and Bach in his *Christmas Oratorio* onwards, used it to invoke precisely that freedom from which it had been rescued. Beethoven wrote a long rustic tune for it in the third movement of his 'Pastoral' Symphony, Berlioz in a pastoral scene in his *Symphonie fantastique*, and the 'Morning' melody from Grieg's *Peer Gynt* suite is unmistakably intended to invoke a calm rural morning. Farmyard animals have also been imitated by the oboe – a crowing cock in Haydn's *The Seasons* and a duck in Prokofiev's *Peter and the Wolf.* There is a lovely oboe solo at the beginning of the second movement of Schubert's 'Great' C major symphony.

The oboe d'amore is intermediate in pitch and size between the cor anglais and the oboe proper. At a distance it is difficult to distinguish from the former as it also has the reed mounted on a metal tube and a pear-shaped end. It is a transposing instrument, and is written a minor third higher than it sounds. It is so little used that many works of reference or about orchestration do not mention it at all. It belongs to a small class of obsolete instruments with small, sweet voices all named d'amore; these include the flute, viola and guitar. Although it is used in Richard Strauss's *Sinfonia Domestica*, Ravel's *Bolero* and Debussy's *Gigues*, its unassertive voice, which is due to the narrow bore, can be hard to distinguish.

Cor anglais (English horn)

With its greater length, curved tube carrying the reed and pear shaped bell, the cor anglais is easily distinguishable from the oboe. Its range is a fifth below that of the oboe, but it is written a fifth higher than it sounds. Thus it is a transposing instrument.

It is hard to believe, from what Rimsky-Korsakov called the 'indolent and dreamy' timbre of this instrument, that it might have originated from an English hunting signal horn – but that is one suggestion about its derivation. Another, disputed and dismissed by most writers, is that the pipe was once angled and should really be called *cor anglé*. A third suggestion is that the name is a mistranslation of *cor angélique* to Englische horn.

Fingering and technique are the same as for the oboe and, as with the oboe, the reed is the 'soul' of the instrument.

The cor anglais was never a regular member of the classical orchestra, particularly the small orchestra. Gluck scored for it occasionally, Beethoven and Weber never. In one symphony only, his 22nd Symphony, 'The Philosopher' (1764), Haydn used two cor anglais instead of oboes. He also used the instrument in chamber and vocal music, however. Incidentally, Haydn authority H.C. Robbins Landon believes that for Haydn it was indeed cor anglé – 'bent horn'.

By the end of the nineteenth century its distinctive timbre was heard in the works of César Franck (1822–1890) and Dvořák (1841–1904); indeed, one of the most famous cor anglais melodies is the tune in the slow movement of Dvořák's 'New World' symphony, which is based on an American spiritual. Berlioz was very pleased with his use of it to express 'sorrowful loneliness' in his *Symphonie fantastique*. The best known passage of all is not in a symphonic work but in the opening of the third act of Wagner's *Tristan and Isolde*, where it performs the role of a lamenting shepherd's pipe.

This is the peasant dance tune from the third movement of Beethoven's 'Pastoral' symphony

Here is the opening of Haydn's 22nd Symphony, 'The Philosopher'. A pair of horns, playing in octaves, make the statement, and a pair of cor anglais (English horns) a lovely response

Oboe and cor anglais repertoire

Beethoven: Symphony No. 6 ('Pastoral')
Schubert: Symphony No. 9 ('Great')
Berlioz: *Symphonie fantastique*
Grieg: *Peer Gynt* suite no. 1
Haydn: *The Seasons*
Prokofiev: *Peter and the Wolf*
Dvořák: Symphony No. 9 ('From the New World')
Wagner: *Tristan and Isolde*
Haydn: Symphony No. 22 ('The Philosopher')

The
Clarinet

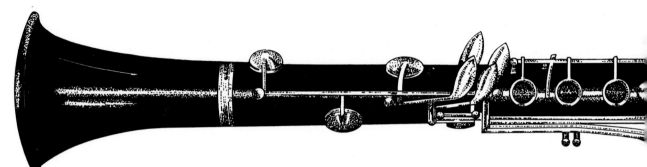

The clarinet part is written in the treble clef on the stave below that of the oboe. It is a transposing instrument with a compass of three octaves and a sixth.

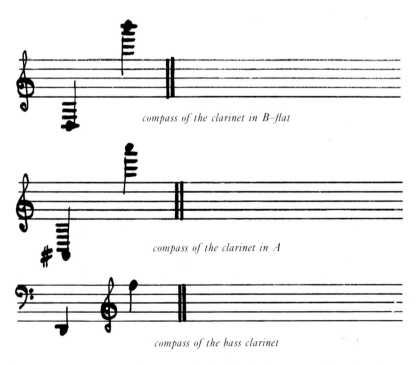

compass of the clarinet in B–flat

compass of the clarinet in A

compass of the bass clarinet

From a distance the vertically-held clarinet resembles the oboe. The distinguishing feature is its beak-shaped mouthpiece with the single reed clamped into position by a metal ligature.

The clarinet has four registers. The lowest is called *chalumeau*, and contains the largest number of uneven partials or harmonics. The *throat* register from G to B flat is considered dull and unworthy of expressing a good tune. The *clarinet* and *extreme* registers are clear and expressive.

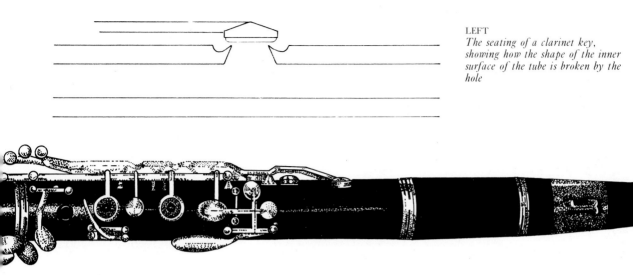

LEFT
The seating of a clarinet key, showing how the shape of the inner surface of the tube is broken by the hole

The clarinet is generally described as being a stopped cylindrical tube, but in fact only roughly two thirds are perfectly cylindrical. Part of the tube leading to the bell is conical, and so is the mouthpiece, which does not hermetically seal the top.

These factors, plus the fact that the surface of the bore of the tube is not perfectly smooth on account of the key holes, all contribute to the complex timbre. Uneven harmonics are present in force in the lower register and diminish in number towards the higher, where even harmonics are present. None the less, the clarinet behaves as though it were a proper stopped cylindrical pipe – which is awkward, for it means that instead of overblowing at the octave, like the flute, it overblows at the twelfth. To produce a chromatic scale on the clarinet 24 or more keys are needed, and still this does not solve the problem of bridging the gap. It is for this reason that many clarinettists still carry with them two instruments, one in A for sharp keys and one in B flat for flat keys. In spite of the two instruments, complex fingering is still involved. There is no uniform system of fingering and one tutor alone liberally offers ten alternative fingerings for one single note.

BELOW
The clarinet disassembled. All woodwind instruments are carried around very safely, disassembled and fitted into their own cases

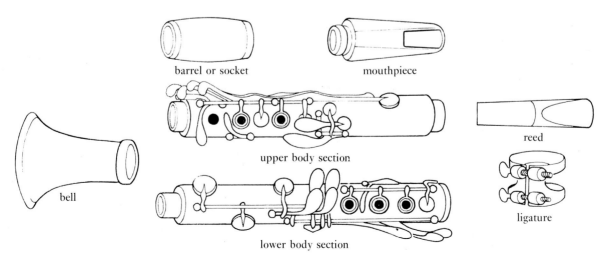

barrel or socket

mouthpiece

reed

upper body section

bell

ligature

lower body section

FAR RIGHT
A dog's life? The Esterházy family were patrons of Haydn, Mozart and Beethoven. In this picture from 1809, an Irish Water Spaniel listens to Prince Nicolaus Esterházy (1765–1833), who plays a clarinet of the period

Woodwind and brass players are frequently asked 'Is your instrument easy to play?' The answer is that all instruments somehow become more difficult as the instrumentalist becomes more experienced.

History

The clarinet arrived relatively late in the orchestra but fairly soon became popular with the best composers. This was due to its interesting expressive qualities and generous dynamic range.

Although cylindrical tubes with single reeds were known to ancient and rustic communities, documentation on these is confused and obscure. Whether the clarinet was developed from the *chalumeau*, a word which could indicate single or double reed pipe, is not known for sure. The name of the instrument may derive from *clarion*, an old French word which referred to some form of clear-sounding wind instrument of the horn or trumpet type: the early clarinet could sound very like a trumpet, and was sometimes written for in clarion-sounding style. In fact military bands adopted the instrument before orchestras. A 17th century family of instrument makers in Nuremburg called Denner is credited with important stages in its early development, even with actually inventing it. Denner's development consisted of adding a speaker key, that is to say an additional hole that made it possible to play in the upper register. Thereafter the history of the instrument consists of an endless series of experiments made with the aim of producing one instrument that could be played chromatically in all keys.

By the beginning of the 18th century there were clarinets with five keys, made in boxwood with ivory mounts; this was the type of instrument which Rameau, Handel, Bach and Gluck wrote for. At the end of the 18th century the orchestral and chamber music repertoire of the clarinet had developed and flourished with a vigour unknown to any other woodwind instrument of that period, and no symphony was without two.

Apart from the A and B flat clarinets only two others of a family of twenty-seven of different sizes, ranging from 14 inches to nearly nine feet in length, are common today; they are the small E flat and the large bass.

RIGHT
The clarinet family. The A and B-flat instruments are the most familiar

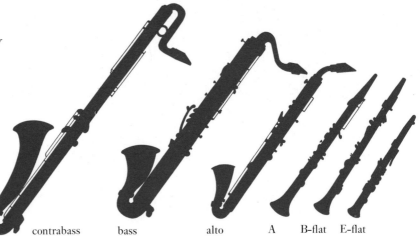

contrabass   bass   alto   A   B-flat E-flat

FAR RIGHT
A bass clarinet and a B-flat clarinet

The E flat clarinet sounds a fourth above the B flat and the bass an octave below. The small E flat has a very penetrating sound wonderfully exploited in a difficult solo by Copland in the ballet *El Salon Mexico*. At first glimpse the bass clarinet could be confused with the saxophone, the bell in both cases being curved upwards and the reed mounted on a curved tube. A saxophone however is all shiny metal, while the body of the bass clarinet is of wood and only the extremities are of metal. It has a noticeably reedy, hole-in-the-middle or hollow sound in the low register and the middle register has something of string quality about it. The works in which it occurs by Meyerbeer and Liszt are not often heard, but the comical side of its character was expressed by Tchaikovsky in the 'Dance of the Sugarplum Fairy' in the *Nutcracker* suite; in this its grave sound is set against the frivolous tinkle of the celesta.

Technique

The single reed of the clarinet is just as much the 'soul' of the instrument as is the double reed of the oboe. Most reed for instruments comes from the Mediterranean, from around Fréjus in particular. After the reed is cut it is seasoned in the open air for two years or more. A well-seasoned reed should be golden and with a straight and evenly-spaced grain; it must neither absorb too much

The woodwind section of an orchestra: a flute and two oboe players are seen in the foregound; in the next row are two clarinets and two bassoons

moisture nor remain rigidly dry. Experiments with synthetic or varnished reeds have proved unsatisfactory. The choice and treatment of reeds varies from player to player, the breadth and the scrape being important factors. By altering lip pressure on the reed the player lengthens or shortens the vibrating portion and alters its natural frequency; this affects the timbre of the instrument. The timbre is also affected by the throat of the player. If the throat is taut and constricted the sound will be pinched. Fingering also affects the timbre of notes. If a note is produced with too much open pipe it will have less character than one coming from a more enclosed tube. A long note may be played with one fingering, while the same note in a rapid passage may well be fingered differently for ease of execution. Degrees of volume are produced by well-supported variations of lung power, but additional projection can be achieved by playing bell up, with the clarinet held forward horizontally or upwards in the manner of jazz musicians, directing the sound into the audience. Single, double, triple and flutter tonguing are all written for, and there is no limit to the leaps and bounds that can be made from one register to another.

Repertoire

The expressive powers of the clarinet are such that its repertoire in chamber, concerto and orchestral music includes works of everlasting importance and value. Mozart, Weber and Brahms were three of the composers who showed a particular fondness for the instrument, the first two writing concerti for it and Brahms his celebrated Clarinet Quintet. Both Mozart and Brahms had the advantage of 'tame' clarinettists as friends, and were therefore influenced and encouraged to write for the instrument.

In a number of familiar overtures the clarinet often captures the attention by some outstanding solo, as towards the end of Mendelssohn's overture *The Hebrides* (Fingal's Cave) and near the beginning of Weber's *Der Freischütz*. Apart from overtures, variations frequently provide a fund of interesting passages for different instruments; Elgar's *Enigma Variations* are particularly rich in exposed passages for the clarinet. Gershwin's *Rhapsody in Blue* begins with a jazz-influenced clarinet glissando.

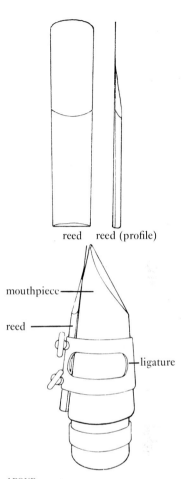

ABOVE
Clarinet, ligature and reed (two views)

FAR LEFT
Alto and soprano saxophones

The B-flat clarinet plays a trill, then a thrilling glissando, in the unmistakable opening of George Gershwin's Rhapsody in Blue, as orchestrated by Ferde Grofé

Clarinet repertoire

Gershwin: *Rhapsody in Blue*
Copland: *El Salon Mexico*
Tchaikovsky: 'Dance of the
   Sugar-Plum Fairy' from the
   Nutcracker
Mozart: Clarinet Concerto
Mozart: Clarinet Quintet
Weber: Clarinet Concerto
Brahms: Clarinet Quintet
Mendelssohn: Overture,
   Midsummer Night's Dream
Weber: Overture, *Der*
   Freischütz
Elgar: *Enigma Variations*

The Saxophone

ABOVE
The saxophone mouthpiece is almost identical to that of the clarinet

RIGHT
Some of the saxophone family are shown here. There is a wide variety of saxophones in different sizes and different keys. Ravel's Boléro, for example calls for a B-flat soprano, a B-flat tenor and a small soprano in F, but this latter part can be played on the soprano, because it does not go very high

soprano   *tenor*   *bass*

The saxophone has to be treated as a family of seven instruments of different sizes, each one covering $2\frac{1}{2}$ octaves and all seven a compass of $5\frac{1}{2}$ octaves. Saxophones look like outsize metal tobacco pipes supported by neck slings, apart from the sopranos which are shorter, parabolic cones. All have a single reed, clarinet-type mouthpiece. Classed as woodwinds, though made of brass, their part is written in a treble clef on a stave beneath the clarinets.

History

Saxophones were named by Adolphe Sax (1814–1894), whose invention they were, and whose father was a fine and imaginative instrument maker. Adolphe studied flute and clarinet at the Brussels Conservatoire. He began by trying to improve the clarinet, in particular in the bass. As has been mentioned, the clarinet overblows at the twelfth and requires much complicated keywork and fingering to produce a satisfactory chromatic scale; by combining the single-reed clarinet mouthpiece with a re-designed tube configuration, Sax was able to produce an instrument that overblows at the octave. This new shape led to simpler keywork, similar to that of the oboe.

The saxophone was invented in 1841, and soon Sax was operating a successful workshop in Paris. French military bands adopted the saxophone in preference to clarinets and bassoons, and Sax began a series of wins at important exhibitions, culminating in 1851 at the Great Exhibition at the Crystal Palace in London's Hyde Park. The next year, however, he was bankrupt; his financial affairs had become hopelessly entangled. By 1877 he had been obliged to sell his much-enlarged Parisian premises; he also sold his collection of instruments, to the Museum of the Paris Conservatoire.

Repertoire

The saxophone has never become a regular member of the orchestra, and at first only the French scored for it, among them Delibes, Saint-Saëns, d'Indy and Bizet. The first, in the 1840s, was Johann Georg Kastner, opera composer and author of the first important French treatise on instrumentation (whose son, incidentally, invented the pyrophone, a weird device which produced singing flames).

In the 20th century, however, partly as a result of its adoption by military bands, the saxophone has become an instrument of primary importance in popular music, especially jazz. Such American players as Johnny Hodges, Lester Young and Charlie Parker on alto, and Ben Webster and Coleman Hawkins on tenor, to name just a few, established the saxophone securely as a means of intensely personal self-expression, relying particularly on its resemblance to the sound of the human voice. It is not surprising, therefore, that 20th century composers have found the occasional appropriate use for it, especially the French, who have been influenced by jazz. Debussy wrote a rhapsody for saxophone and piano which has been orchestrated; Ravel used it in his *Bolero*, and in his masterful orchestration of Mussorgsky's *Pictures at an Exhibition*, where he assigned it the role of the troubadour singing to gain entrance to 'The Old Castle'. The Germans ignored the instrument until Richard Strauss introduced a quartet into his *Symphonia Domestica*. Curiously, Vaughan Williams, who was not a great orchestrator and reportedly sought advice on the subject, not only wrote a concerto for tuba and a romance for the harmonica, but also used a saxophone in his ballet *Job*. And there is an alto saxophone part in the *Dies Irae* of Britten's *Sinfonia da Requiem*, which was written in 1940 during the Second World War, the subject of the work.

In Maurice Ravel's orchestration of Mussorgsky's Pictures at an Exhibition, the alto saxophone plays *the part of a troubadour singing this plaintive melody at the gate of 'The Old Castle'*

Saxophone repertoire

Ravel: Rhapsody for
  Saxophone
Ravel: *Bolero*
Mussorgsky–Ravel: 'The Old
  Castle' from *Pictures at an
  Exhibition*
Strauss: *Symphonia Domestica*
Vaughan Williams: *Job*
Britten: *Dies Irae* from *Sinfonia
  da Requiem*

The
Bassoon

compass of the bassoon

compass of the contrabassoon

The bassoon has a compass of $3\frac{1}{2}$ octaves. It is written for in a bass or tenor clef on a stave in between the clarinet and the horn.

This large woodwind instrument, usually made of maple, can be identified by the fact that it is held diagonally across the body, supported by a neck sling or sometimes by a floor spike in the butt or bottom of the tubing. The longish, curved crook that carries the double reed is another distinguishing feature. The sound has different characteristics in different registers, but in legato passages in the upper register the sound has been compared to that of the human voice, and therefore has been called *vox humana*. The lower register has a solemn, even ponderous quality which when given rapid staccato passages can sound comical, the effect being of an elephant trying to dance like a gnat.

With reed and crook the total bore-length of the instrument is about 9ft $2\frac{1}{4}$ inches. The bassoon can be dismantled into five parts; the matching grain for all the components is important not only to the appearance but to the sound, since knotted wood of unmatched grain

ABOVE
*A bassoonist of the BBC
Symphony Orchestra*

ABOVE
*The contrabassoon has its weight
taken to the floor by a spike, like a
cello*

A detail from the title page of the
Syntagma Musicum of Michael
Praetorius. In the loft are cornetts,
organ and conductor; and below them
in a panel various instruments are
represented: flute, curtal, shawm
and crumhorn

RIGHT
This simplified drawing of the 'wing'
of a bassoon shows how the holes are
drilled diagonally

would not make a good sound conductor. Some cheap bassoons are today made of synthetic material, but no synthetic ever produces as interesting and rich a sound as the natural material.

History

The bassoon is so called on account of its low voice. In scores it is called the fagotto, fagott or fagotte, referring to the fact that the tubes are bound together, not to its resemblance to a bundle of wood, the word for which comes from the same French root.

The most recent and exhaustive book on the bassoon, by Lyndesay G. Langwill, states that 'The origin of the bassoon is still shrouded in mystery. Even its country of origin is uncertain.' A degree of confidence is however expressed in the belief that the bassoon's immediate ancestor was the curtal. But since 'curtal' has at various times been spelled corthol, curtail, curtil and curtall, and confused with the fagottino and the phagotum, quite apart from the courtaut and the cervelat (which is also the name for a short, fat sausage), it can be appreciated that nomenclature, far from clarifying, adds to the confusion. The evocative names bombard, brummer and pommer are also implicated in the murky mystery of origins, some scholars having declared that the curtal is a curtailed pommer. For those seeking further clarification (or more confusion) on instruments of the 17th century two sources are worth careful study: the first is the *Syntagma musicum* (1615–19) by Michael Praetorius and the second, already mentioned, is *Harmonie Universelle* (1636–7) by Father Marin Mersenne. Both include illustrations of the early bassoon, showing it to be made from one block of wood and therefore not truly fagotted. Even at this period it had keys. Another and later source, used for entertainment rather than for accuracy, is *The Showcase of Musical Instruments* by Filippo Bonanni, first published in 1723 and recently republished in both Britain and the U.S. Here there is an illustration of a fagotto, described as a bassoon in the text, which shows a moony young man blowing into a long tube with enormous holes which his elegant fingers could not possibly close; their spacing would be equally unmanageable. The fact is that one of the unique features of bassoon construction, and one that is a major contributory factor to the timbre of the instrument, is the holes. A large, long tube needs large holes, which cannot be covered by normal human finger tips anyway, so the holes of the bassoon have always been bored obliquely. Partly as a result of this, partials or harmonics in the sound are stronger than the fundamental, and it can happen that some listeners hear only those upper partials and are led to believe that they are misreading the score, or that the bassoonist is playing the wrong notes.

In common with other wind instruments the bassoon gradually acquired more keys from the 17th century onwards. The parts were then separately bored, turned and fagotted with metal hoops. But it was discovered that too much tampering with the configuration of the U-shaped tube and obliquely bored holes altered the timbre of the instrument too radically, so after about the middle of the 19th century little more was done to 'improve' it. By then it was in any case a valued member of the symphony orchestra.

It is believed that it was first introduced into the orchestra in France by a then-sensational composer and hated rival of Lully, Robert Cambert. Cambert was the originator of French opera and it was in *Pomone* (1671) that he included the voice of the bassoon in the score.

Because they are both double reed instruments, the oboe and the bassoon are sometimes described together, as though the former were simply a complement in compass to the latter. But this is not so, as the position of the bassoon in the score must show. In the 18th century it was used to double with cellos, and its presence was so much taken for granted that bassoon parts were not even written out, it being assumed the bassoonists would be present and ready to double. In the 19th century it gradually won a more independent role and was acclaimed as 'the gentleman of the orchestra'.

Technique

Double reed players have a habit of blowing their reeds divorced from the instrument and producing Mickey Mouse sounds, called croaks or crows. These sounds are made in order to establish the frequency or pitch of the individual reed, and for the bassoon this should be between F and G sharp. Most bassoons are sold with two crooks, one

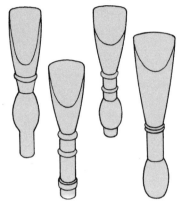

ABOVE
A selection of bassoon reeds, showing different scrapes

RIGHT
Bassoonists of the Chicago Symphony Orchestra

being shorter and therefore sharper than the other. Which combination of reed and crook is used for which instrument and what music will depend on the player.

The production of clean and accurate notes on the bassoon is notoriously difficult partly on account of the large size of the double reed, which is held in the mouth. This makes double tonguing difficult. Triple tonguing is hardly ever used. Intonation is adjusted by lip pressure on the reed, but if the reed or sound holes clog with moisture, the instrument sounds like a punctured air bed, and the 'gentleman of the orchestra' becomes the clown.

Bassoonists can sometimes be observed blowing discreetly into the key holes of their instruments to clear the moisture. There is also a water key in the butt end to drain off accumulated condensation. Reeds have to be washed, and crooks cleaned with a bristle brush. And most bassoonists will carry the odd elastic band for immediate emergency repairs in the event of a spring breaking.

As there are different key systems for different bassoons, so there are various methods of cross-fingering which themselves may be adapted to suit a particular bassoon. Even though a series of bassoons may come from the same maker, each will have a distinct character of its own. And while many instrumentalists will, in a crisis, be able to transfer from one instrument to a substitute and play with a fair amount of success, if also a good deal of grumbling, bassoonists cannot do this. The difference between one instrument and another is too great.

Repertoire

Orchestral music abounds with effective passages for bassoon, such as the second movement of Bartók's *Concerto for Orchestra*. Although the bassoon is frequently used to provide comical effects, such as the 'Dance of the Clowns' in Mendelssohn's incidental music for *A Midsummer Night's Dream*, its repertoire includes many richly expressive passages particularly for the *vox humana* register. This can be heard in the waltz in Tchaikovsky's Fifth Symphony and in Stravinsky's *Rite of Spring*. Greig gives the bassoon the theme in the 'Morning' section of his *Peer Gynt* suite, as does Dukas in *L'Apprenti Sorcier*. Beethoven scored generously for the bassoon in all his symphonies, using the double or contrabassoon as well in the Fifth and the Ninth. Weber and Mozart each wrote a bassoon concerto and Vivaldi wrote 37 of them. The human voice quality of the timbre was also used by Mozart in certain of his operas to accompany the voice, and in Prokofiev's *Peter and the Wolf* the bassoon actually performs the part of the grandfather's voice.

In Dukas' tone poem, the Sorceror's Apprentice gets up to mischief while the master is out of the room. He casts a spell to make the broom carry the water, but then he cannot break the spell, and the room is soon awash. The bassoon, jaunty and single-minded, plays the part of the broom

Bassoon repertoire

Bartók: *Concerto for Orchestra*
Mendelssohn: 'Dance of the Clowns', incidental music for *Midsummer Night's Dream*
Dukas: *L'Apprenti Sorcier*
Prokofiev: *Peter and the Wolf*
Stravinsky: *Rite of Spring*
Grieg: *Peer Gynt* suite no. 1
Tchaikovsky: Symphony No. 5

THE
BRASS
INSTRUMENTS

The French Horn

compass of the French horn in F

Horn parts are written in treble and bass clefs without key signature, accidentals being written in as they occur. The horn is a transposing instrument and sounds a fifth lower than written in the treble clef but a fourth higher in the bass clef.

In his book on the French horn Morley Pegge described the sound of the instrument as 'the most refined and poetical voice in the symphony orchestra'. Its emotional range certainly covers the moods from martial to melancholy.

A description of the appearance of this noble brass instrument and its timbre seems unnecessary. Technically it has the misfortune to be classed as a 'lip vibrated aerophone'. The principles of sound production are the same as for reed instruments, but in this case it is the vibration of the player's lips within the funnel of the mouthpiece, not a reed, which sets the long column of coiled air vibrating. The rate of vibration is controlled by the tension of the lip muscles: high tension for high notes, slack muscles for low notes. Experiments to produce sound in this way can be made by anyone with a length of pipe, be it hose, drain or watering-can spout. The range of notes or harmonics that can be produced from these tubes will depend not only on the lip of the performer but on the size and configuration of any mouthpiece which acts as a form of funnel, directing and controlling the quantity of air.

History

Horns are a symbol of power and strength as were the horned beasts – elephants, bulls and boars – from which they were first made. At first these horns were used as signalling instruments, principally for hunters of anything from the stag to the hare and the fox. Messages

A small 17th century hunting horn by the celebrated Parisian maker R. Crétien, with a beautifully engraved garland

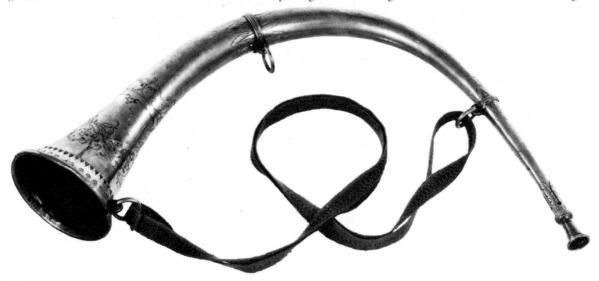

A pre-valve horn with case and crooks, made by L.R. Raoux, the most notable maker of horns in the late 18th century

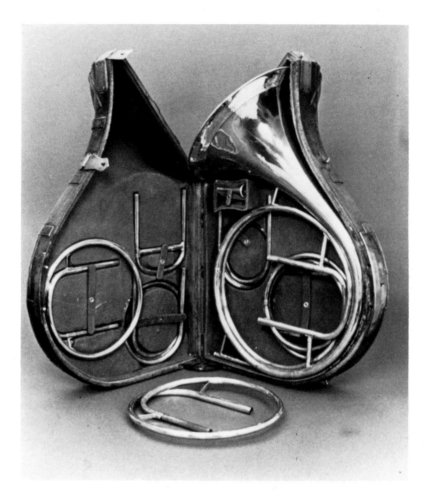

about sightings and killings were conveyed by series of rhythmic codes which gradually became more elaborate and developed into tunes based on the harmonic series. For early theatre- and opera-goers one blast on a horn or two and they knew they were in for a merry hunting scene. The shapes and sizes of those early horns varied, but the hooped *cor de chasse* is no doubt the one from which the orchestral one derives. It is called French by English speaking people because that is its country of origin; it is called plain *cor* by the French.

The history of the development of the horn from the 17th century onwards can be divided into four main stages, throughout which the objective was to produce a chromatic instrument.

One length of coiled tubing can produce only one set of harmonics – that gapped scale of very unequal temperament. At first additional lengths of tubing called crooks were used to extend the compass. By the end of the 18th century there were individual crooks for every key. Crooks were very impractical on account of having to carry all the heavy ironmongery about, and also because of having to change crooks mid-music if there was a change of key or an accidental. Up to this period the sound of the horn was considered coarse and vulgar. Then something happened which promoted it 'at one bound from the stables to the drawing room' (Morley Pegge).

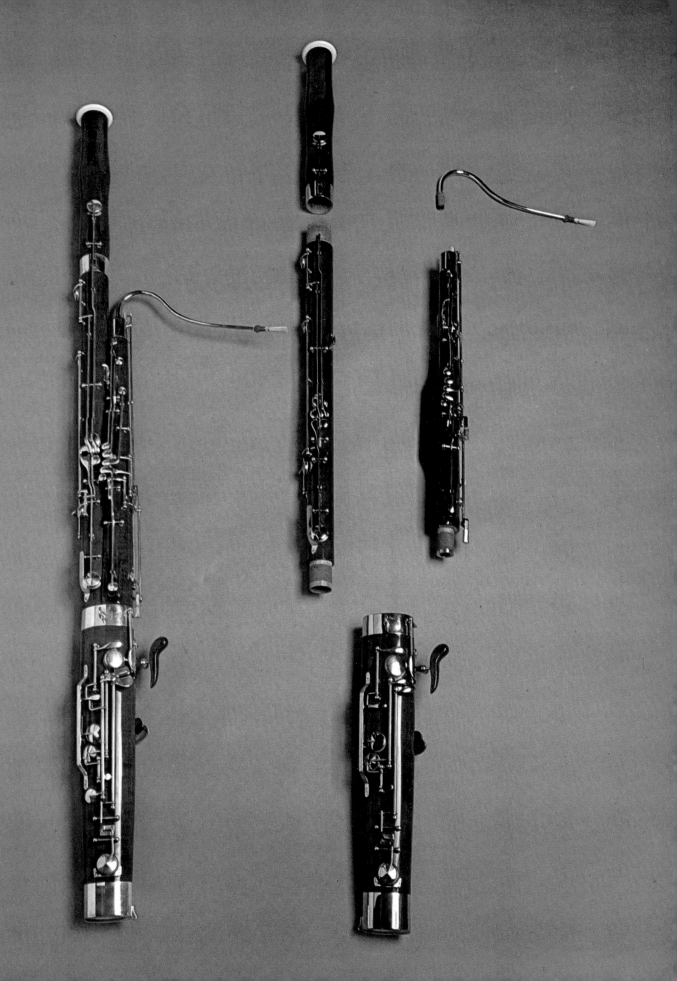

At this period the oboe sound was also considered coarse and vulgar, and sometimes a wad of cotton was stuffed up the globular bell to sweeten the voice. In about 1770 a horn player of Dresden, Hampl (or Hampel), who was in any case tired of changing crooks, used the same method to refine the sound of the horn and discovered that this altered the fundamental and provided another set of harmonics. The further the cotton plug was inserted up the bell, the lower the pitch until, at a certain distance, the pitch rose by a semitone. Hampl then dispensed with the cotton plug and used his hand instead. Thus the hand horn was invented.

All the sound from the horn flows out of the bell and therefore anything impeding this flow will affect the timbre, as well as the pitch. With the hand horn some notes were stopped, others were open, and there was a difference in quality between the two. There is a curious convention in music which relates any particular beautiful or haunting sound to creatures of another world; thus these hand-stopped notes have been described as elf-like. Composers were very pleased with the contrast between worldly and unworldly timbre, but Hampl was not; he set about re-designing the horn in order to overcome the contrast. He made the mouthpiece funnel- instead of cup-shaped and introduced slides to provide adjustments to pitch. This type of horn was written for until the latter part of the 19th century, in spite of the introduction of the valve horn, which was a major breakthrough but was treated with some reserve by many composers.

The French horn is today held with the hand in the bell, but not always for the purpose of changing the length of the air column. Who invented the valve horn in the early 19th century is open to question, but the name Heinrich Stölzel is the one most associated with it. There are two types of valve used on brass instruments, both with the same function of opening and closing different lengths of tubing and producing different sets of harmonics: the piston valve and the rotary. The piston valve is operated by a finger button which depresses a sort of plunger. The rotary valve is a disk operated by a finger plate which opens or closes the air courses. Valves did away with hand stopping but they also did away with 'elf-like' sounds and truly brilliant open notes. Once the vibrating air within the tube had to negotiate sharp bends –

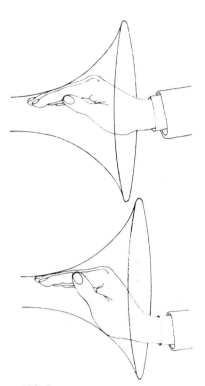

ABOVE
The modern double horn is a chromatic instrument but the player still uses his hand in the bell to refine the tone

FAR LEFT
A modern double horn

LEFT
This drawing shows how the air is re-directed in the horn by a piston valve (left) and a rotary valve (right). The rotor is more common on the modern horn

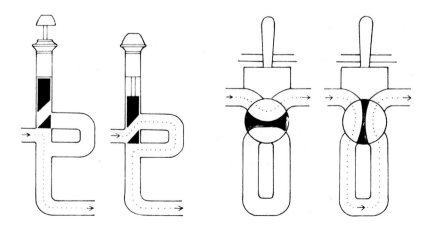

Piston horn, now in a London museum

perhaps even a series of them – the movement of the excited air from the mouthpiece to the bell lost a certain degree of impetus. But at least the horn could be played in any key and hand-stopped notes were still possible, though of different quality.

The ultimate in horn development is the double horn. This dates from the end of the last century and it can be distinguished from the ordinary valve horn by the additional number of twists and turns in the tubing. This is, as the name implies, a combination of sufficient lengths of loops for the instrument to be tuned in either F – like the ordinary valve horn – or B flat alto, giving additional high notes.

The interesting fact about the development of most wind instruments is that when they came in from the field, their sounds were considered unsuitably strident or rough for indoor music and their tones were softened, but when orchestras and concert halls grew in size their volume had to be increased again, so that by the end of the

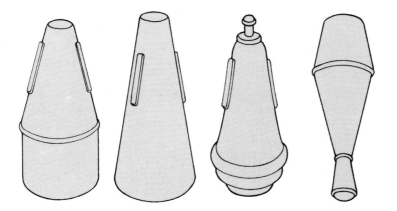

LEFT
A selection of horn mutes

19th century the timbre of the full orchestra bore little or no relation to that of Beethoven's time and earlier. It is for this sort of reason that so many instrumentalists of today, guided by scholars, are interested in playing and recording early orchestral music on the instruments for which it was written.

Technique

The expression 'stiff upper lip' might have originated among brass players because they all must have one. The mouthpiece is held against the upper lip, and the muscles of and around the lips control the pitch. Should the lip become tired it will 'go' and notes will split or crack. Refinements of pitch and timbre are also produced by adjustments of the hand in the bell. But a trembling upper lip and gapped teeth will not produce good horn playing.

Correct fingering does not by itself produce the right note. The horn player has to 'hear' his note before he plays it and adjust lip tension accordingly. A slack lip for a high note would produce a low sound of some sort.

A mute is an essential part of a horn player's equipment, for although a form of muting can be produced by the hand, the mute that can be inserted will produce a different sound. Some mutes are designed with air outlets so that the pitch is not affected; others are airtight and do affect the pitch. The opposite of the muted sound is the *son cuivré*, a blaring or brassy sound produced by overblowing when the hand or mute is inserted.

Trills, tremolos, flutter tonguing and glissandi are all part of the horn repertoire.

Horn players can be observed tipping their instruments and pouring out water. This is condensation and it is released by a water key – a sort of draining device.

The Repertoire

The stages .of technical development of the horn can often be distinguished by the way it is written for. Where the earliest music, such as Handel's *Water Music*, declares its derivation from the *cor de chasse* codes, that of the late 19th century and after display chromatic instruments with a small but interesting variety of different timbres.

All the same, the horn's musical symbolism as an instrument of the hunt, playing rhythmical passages based on the harmonic series, has never been totally abandoned. In 'The Royal Hunt and Storm' from *The Trojans* Berlioz uses it to evoke two planes of perspective – near and distant – as well as in a supporting role.

Mozart (1756–1791) already treated the horn as a melodic instrument, as his horn concerti and Divertimenti alone reveal. And in most of his scores he wrote for two horns, showing great sensitivity to the difference between stopped and open notes. Beethoven (1770–1827) was considered 'singularly cruel and exacting' in his writing for the horn and even in the late 19th century his Sextet for String Quartet and Two Horns obbligato was considered almost unplayable. Weber (1786–1826) wrote one of the most celebrated horn passages in the opening bars of his *Oberon* overture, but to express the

Rotary valve horns of the
Bournemouth Sinfonietta

In the opening of Brahms' Second Piano Concerto, two horns in B-flat state the theme, while the piano answers

'elf-like' atmosphere this should properly be played on the hand horn, as indeed should also the horn solo that opens the Nocturne in Mendelssohn's *Midsummer Night's Dream.*

Rossini (1792–1868), a horn player himself, represents a stage in the new-style writing for the valve horn; Grove's *Dictionary of Music and Musicians* of 1889 remarked rather sniffily that his works were 'abundantly strewn' with runs, turns and scales and treacherous passages that were possible only on this new-fangled machine. There was in fact fairly widespread dismay when the hand horn began to be replaced by the valve horn. In his early years Wagner scored for both together – there is an example in the second act of *The Flying Dutchman* – but *Tristan and Isolde* is scored for hand horns only because Wagner recognized that with the valve horn there was a loss of 'some of (the horn's) beauty of tone and power in producing a smooth legato'.

Although the valve horn was available in Brahms' day (1833–1897), he scored for the hand horn, and his Second Piano Concerto begins with a dialogue between horn and piano. Throughout his symphonies he gives the horns passages of considerable prominence. Towards the turn of the century Richard Strauss (1864–1949), Mahler (1860–1911), Debussy (1862–1918) and others wrote passages extending the range of the horn. Glissandi became fairly common (Mahler called for them in no fewer than three of his symphonies) and flutter tonguing was introduced. The different timbres were also increasingly exploited. In only seven bars of Debussy's *Prélude à l'Après-midi d'un Faune* there are four changes of timbre.

Among the most famous of all melodic passages for the horn are those to be heard in the slow movement of Tchaikovsky's Fifth Symphony, and in Ravel's *Pavane pour une Infante Défunte.*

Horn repertoire

Handel: *Water Music*
Berlioz: 'The Royal Hunt and Storm' from *The Trojans*
Mozart: Horn Concerti (4)
Weber: Overture, *Oberon*
Mendelssohn: 'Nocturne', incidental music for *Midsummer Night's Dream*
Brahms: Piano Concerto No. 2
Mahler: Symphony No. 3
Debussy: *Prélude à l'Après-midi d'un Faune*
Ravel: *Pavane pour une Infante Défunte*
Tchaikovsky: Symphony No. 5

The Trumpet

The part for the trumpet is written on the stave immediately below that of the horns. Whether it is written for as it actually sounds or as a transposing instrument depends on the period of the music, the pitch of the trumpet and on the habit or preference of the composer.

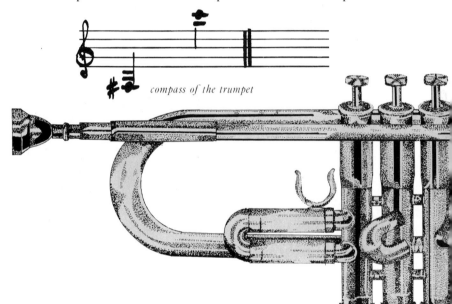

compass of the trumpet

The burnished physical appearance and the sound of this looped and narrow bore instrument are familiar and not likely to be confused with the shorter and wider cornet, because the cornet's less noble tones are not often heard in the symphony orchestra (although Franck included it in his symphony). The cupped mouthpiece of the trumpet is held against the mouth, the lips acting as a form of reed. The right hand fingers the three valves, which are more commonly of the piston type. There is a water key for spilling out condensation on the front of the lower loop. The wrapped tube terminates in a bell the garland of which is often stamped or engraved with the name of the maker. The high gloss is, as with other brass instruments, maintained by a coat of transparent lacquer.

History

The word trumpet is a diminutive of *trumpe*, a larger instrument which, according to certain specialists, will have the privilege of announcing the Last Judgement. In Chaucer's 14th century the trumpet was called *beme* to distinguish it from the large trumpe and the smaller *clarioun*. The root of the word comes from the Greek *strombos*, sea shell.

The history of the trumpet has at least one unusual feature. While most instruments of the orchestra gained in stature and interest when they came out of the cold into the concert hall, the trumpet did not. Previously it had held an elevated and respected role in the highest society, with an interesting repertoire; when admitted to the orchestra the trumpet declined into the obscurity of pronouncing banal clichés, doubling and low grade filling-in. Berlioz expressed the whole sorry slither in his *Treatise on Modern Instrumentation and Orchestration*: 'Notwithstanding the real loftiness and distinguished nature of its quality of tone, there are few instruments that have been more degraded than the trumpet. Down to Beethoven and Weber, every

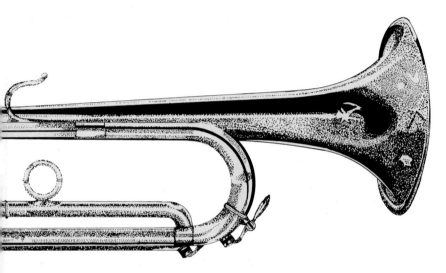

BELOW
A close-up of the trumpeter's fingers on the piston valves

composer – not excepting Mozart – persisted in confining it to the unworthy function of filling up, or in causing it to sound two or three commonplace rhythmical formulae . . . This detestable practice is at last abandoned.' Indeed, a glimpse at the scores of Beethoven's 'Eroica' Symphony or *Egmont* overture will at once show how boring the life of an orchestral trumpeter could be in classical music.

The high status and associations with magical power that the trumpet enjoyed in antiquity was not confined to Europe but was widespread. The earliest pictorial representation of the true trumpet with a narrow cylindrical bore dates from about 2200 BC. Early instruments are usually discovered or depicted in pairs. This has sometimes been interpreted as of purely magical significance, but since it has been found that each instrument of the pair was of different length, it may be simply that the ancients had a good grasp of the harmonic series and that the pairing was a method of obtaining a larger number of notes. (On the other hand, the phenomenon of harmony itself may have had religious significance.) 'Tut's toots', as the BBC Sound Archive staff called recordings of those trumpets discovered in Tutankhamun's tomb, are an example: one blows a whole tone lower than the other.

The evidence of paired trumpets employed in sacred, sacrificial and other special rites and ceremonies abounds from the time of the 14th century BC when the invention of the trumpet was ascribed to the god Osiris, a deity symbolising good and sunlight. Thereafter trumpets were increasingly associated with the panoply of special events, including warfare; the Celts are reported to have blasted the courage out of the enemy by the sound of their carnyx, a form of trumpet terminating in a carved figure of a boar's head. Later, the Islamic world shouted with multitudes of trumpets. In fact no cultivated community or race was ever without trumpeters – there are still State Trumpeters in Britain today.

The elegant aspect of the early straight trumpet was something to hang banners on, which is what happened in the princely and ducal courts of Europe in the early 13th century. Soon the instrument was made S-shaped for easier handling; the centre of gravity was thus shifted and the stance of the player became one degree less elegant. As the centuries passed the centre of gravity was moved to a few inches in front of the player's face, until he could sit down and play.

But back in the 15th century trumpeters had become such snobs that they organized themselves into guilds to protect their near-sacred rights and to limit the activities of such common players as watchmen. They claimed the exclusive right to play at feasts, processions and pageants and were, in large numbers, in the regular pay of sovereigns. Henry VII and Elizabeth I each maintained a dozen or more. And it was at the time of the formation of those guilds that an important distinction was made among trumpeters, a distinction that was to last until the time of Bach and then fizzle out, leaving future generations with a puzzle: exactly what instrument did Bach write his florid trumpet parts for?

Before Bach, trumpeters were classified as principals and clarino players, the former playing in the lower register with its widely-

FAR LEFT
Celtic warriors of the 1st century BC playing the carnyx. It is said that the mouths of the animal heads sometimes contained tongues which, when agitated by the air blown up the trumpet, added to the frightening quality of the sound. This scene is from the Gundestrup cauldron, a large embossed silver vessel found in Denmark

RIGHT
One of a series of woodcuts by Tobias Stimmer (1539–1584) showing women musicians, probably of the nobility. In the original this instrument is called a clarion, and possibly has a sliding joint. 'For war, nothing better was ever invented,' says the poem, 'to make even the horses spring cheerfully into battle.' The only complete set of these woodcuts is in the New York Public Library

stepped harmonics, the latter in the high register where the harmonics lie close together. Shanks and crooks were already used as early as 1600 and by the end of the 18th century there were crooks for every key. These altered the timbre of the instrument, and there was some degree of energy loss as the vibrating air column negotiated the loops. Then came the valves, introducing more loops, and someone writing at the time of their application, towards the end of the 19th century, described them as 'a failure as they obscure the upper harmonics, the main source of characteristic tone'. Berlioz however thought they produced the truest intervals. Berlioz and Wagner both accepted the

RIGHT
This simplified drawing of the trumpet shows the re-direction of the air by means of the piston valve

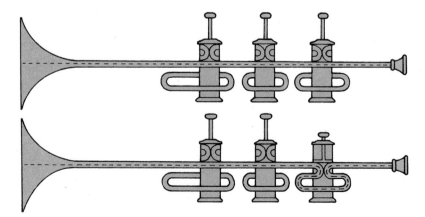

valve trumpet and were largely responsible for developing its importance as an instrument of the symphony orchestra.

To return to the mystery of 'the Bach trumpet' as it is called, meaning the one that can play high register florid passages: in earlier centuries patrons and the public wished to hear the very latest and most up-to-date music and there was none of today's eager curiosity about music of the past, nor fear of contemporary music. When Bach died in 1750 popular interest in his music waned. A hundred or so years later when Mendelssohn resurrected those 'noble relics of the past', as they were then considered, clarino playing and the instrument on which it had been done no longer existed. The search therefore began for 'the Bach trumpet'. It is discouraging to find that, in spite of the number of clarino players there must have been, only one of the sort of trumpets they used has been identified, and a number of different substitutes have been tried out, since different ideas prevail about the quality of timbre of the Bach trumpet.

Technique

The quality of timbre produced by wind players is much affected by the air cavities in the head, throat and chest; these are forms of resonators. A trumpeter may not be taught to use these, but he will certainly learn to. The cup mouthpiece is not rammed against the lips, but held firmly so that when the piston valves are worked the trumpet is not joggled. The physical wind pressure exerted by brass players exceeds that of all other wind instrument players and therefore long passages with little breathing space can be punishing to perform. High passages require a taut lip and can cause muscle fatigue; the lip can 'go' producing a spray of cracked notes. Intonation is not purely a matter of lip control. There is always the problem of the rising temperature of the concert hall; this expands metal and raises the pitch of the instrument. And during long periods when the trumpet has no part to play the metal cools off and the instrument falls below pitch. Tuning up at the start of a concert is as much a warming up.

All trumpeters carry one mute or more, the ordinary one that muffles the tone being the most common. With and without mute, extremely rapid tonguing, glissandi and great leaps are all possible, as well as trills and turns.

BELOW
A selection of trumpet mutes

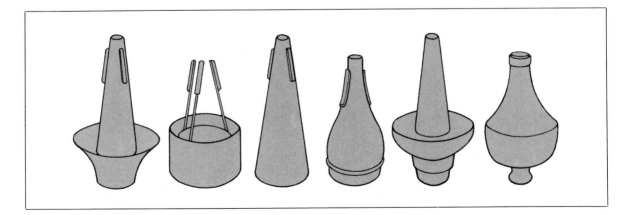

Repertoire

Before the 17th century most trumpet music belonged to the oral tradition and was not written down. This was one method of ensuring that guild members kept all their secrets to themselves. Until the middle of the 17th century fanfares were the most common currency. In the early 18th century, with its clarino players, the agility and the compass of the trumpet was presumed to match that of the human voice, and J.S. Bach's Brandenburg Concerto No. 2 contains a trumpet part that is equal in brilliance to that of the flute.

There is, of course, a trumpet concerto by Haydn from 1796 (written for a keyed trumpet) and the famous little 'Trumpet Voluntary' by Jeremiah Clarke (d.1707) (originally written for the trumpet stop on the organ). But in the classical period trumpeters were generally reduced to having more bars to count than to play, even in the symphonies of Beethoven. He wrote one of the most celebrated passages for trumpet, to be played off stage, in the overture *Leonora No. 3*, which is often used as an *entr'acte* in the opera *Fidelio*. Even this, though more subtle than the passage for trumpets in Rossini's *William Tell Overture*, is essentially a military announcement. The resurrection of the trumpet can be said to have begun with Wagner –

BELOW
The trumpet section of the Bournemouth Sinfonietta

note his overture to *Rienzi* – and Elliot Carter's *Symphony for Three Orchestras*, premiered in 1979, begins with a totally chromatic trumpet solo which is very striking.

Although trumpets and trumpeters in this century do not enjoy the privileges of the past, at least the instrument has gained a wide popularity on account of its use in dance, jazz and brass bands. Indeed, Louis Armstrong, starting on cornet, became the first and greatest solo star in all of popular music, and has influenced the use of the trumpet in orchestral music.

LEFT
The trumpet is not very often the star in the symphony orchestra, but the prestige it had in earlier times has been regained in popular music. In 1925, at the beginning of the electrical recording process, Louis Armstrong (1900–1971) began making an incandescent series of recordings which made him one of the first big solo stars in the history of the gramophone record

In Mussorgsky's Pictures at an Exhibition, Ravel assigned the opening statement of the 'Promenade' theme to the trumpet – solo at first, but joined after two bars by the other two trumpets, as well as horns and tuba. The tune depicts the composer *wandering from picture to picture at an exhibition of drawings by his late friend, architect and designer Victor Hartmann. It recurs throughout the suite of pieces, originally written for the piano*

Trumpet repertoire

Bach: Brandenburg Concerto
No. 2
Haydn: Trumpet Concerto
Clarke: Trumpet Voluntary
Beethoven: Overture, *Leonora No. 3*
Rossini: Overture, *William Tell*
Carter: *Symphony for Three Orchestras*

The Trombone

In the score the music for the trombone is written in a bass or tenor clef on the stave over and sometimes beneath that of the timpani. The compass is two octaves and a sixth. The sound, produced by means of a shallow cupped mouthpiece which is lip vibrated, is powerful and rich in harmonics.

these compasses exclude pedal notes:

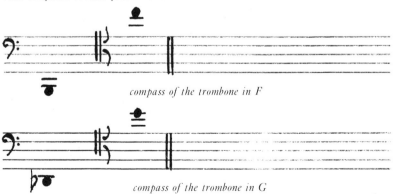

compass of the trombone in F

compass of the trombone in G

The trombone is the only naturally chromatic wind instrument in the orchestra. The long cylindrical tube has only two bends or bows, one terminating in the bell and the other in the mouthpiece. The instrument is held up almost horizontally in front of the player. The forward portion of the U-shaped tubing is telescopic; this the player holds with his right hand, sliding it in and out to shorten or lengthen the air column, thereby obtaining a series of different fundamentals and sets of harmonics.

History

The name is the augmentative of tromba and the trombone is the largest instrument in this family. Earlier it was called the *sackbut*, sometimes written *saggbutt*. The etymological derivation of this earlier name is in doubt. One early 18th century dictionary charmingly but inaccurately explains that it is '*sacabuche* – to fetch the Breath from the bottom of the Belly because it requires strong Breath' – which of course it does. But the word could come from a Spanish root describing a type of pump, or, most probably, from the French *sacqueboute*, a lance with a hook used to unseat riders in battle (Old French: *saquier*, to draw out, and *bouter*, to push.)

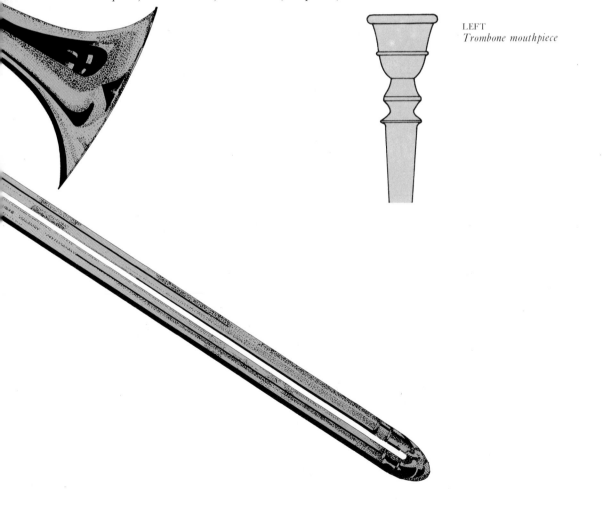

LEFT
Trombone mouthpiece

ABOVE
*A detail from the title page of the
Syntagma Musicum of Michael
Praetorius. The ancestor of the
modern trombone is seen on the left,
the organ in the middle and the
curtal (early bassoon) on the right*

FAR RIGHT
A trumpet

The sackbut was well known in the early 14th century. In appearance it differs little from the modern trombone and the technique of playing has therefore remained unchanged, although quicker slide technique has been developed.

The sackbut was a popular member of the bands of kings and princes and was played at all manner of rituals, ceremonials and feasts. Then it was often played in consort with the cornett – a small curved horn pierced with finger holes whose sound was appreciated for its wonderful resemblance to that of the human voice. The sackbut was written for by Gabrieli (1557–1612) and Monteverdi (1567–1643), but its full potential as a chromatic instrument was not exploited until later. Neither sackbuts nor trombones – as they were soon called – were written for as solo instruments but always in groups of four to eight. 'A single trombone seems out of place. The instrument needs harmony . . .' wrote Berlioz, although Mozart included an obbligato in his *Requiem*. Today the normal complement of the symphony orchestra is two tenor and a bass.

The timbre as well as the role of the sackbut was different in the 15th and 16th centuries. It had thicker walls and a narrower bore; the bell was less flared and the mouthpiece was shallower. The result was a softer voice and, at the risk of over-emphasizing this characteristic of early instruments, it had a more human sound. It was much used to support plainsong in churches, its ability to sound microtones being ideal where subtle church modes were concerned. This role of

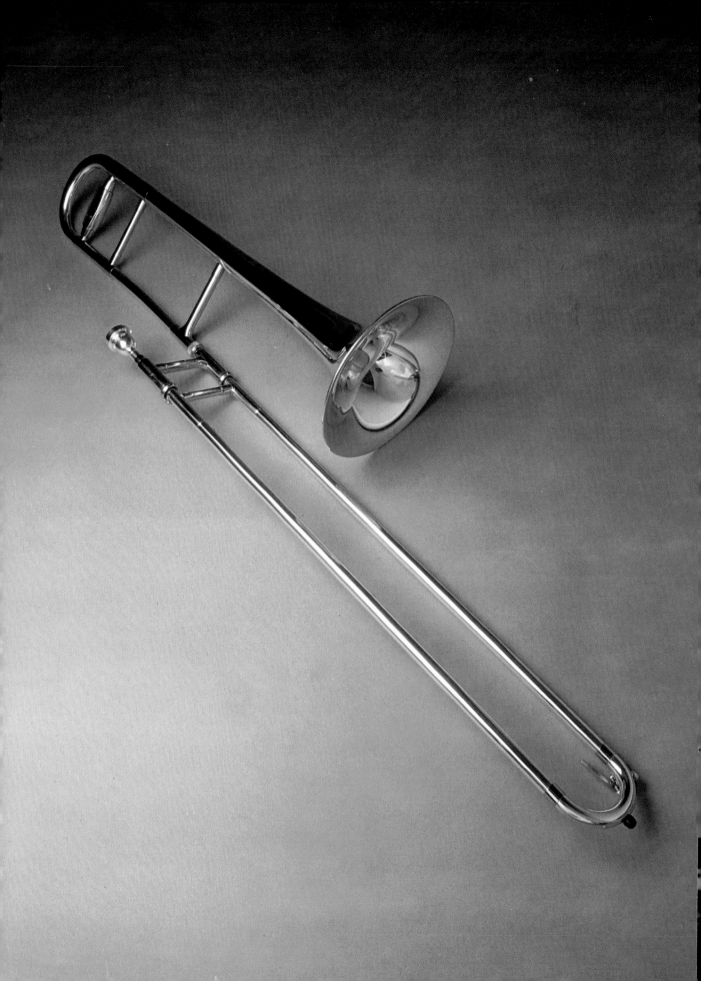

supporting vocal music continued down the centuries from Monteverdi to Mozart and Dvořák and was not unknown in church choirs in England at the end of the last century. Both Bach and Handel used the trombone to double the vocal line.

It might seem obvious that an instrument of such simple and ideal acoustical design would need no improving, but when the day of the piston valve arrived in the early 19th century, it was inevitable that attempts should be made to apply it to the trombone. These were a failure. The first valves were applied in about 1820, but it was discovered that wrapping a long, narrow cylindrical tube into too many tight loops altered the timbre of the instrument too drastically. In an article of 1889 in Grove's *Dictionary of Music and Musicians*, the author, a trombonist, doesn't mention the valve trombone at all. (He does however compensate by offering the following passage of memorable historical information: 'A band composed exclusively of Trombones has been formed, and it is stated to have been particularly fine. It was attached to the elder Wombwell's show of wild beasts.')

LEFT
A sackbut by the 18th century Swiss maker Jacob Steimer

FAR LEFT
A trombone

Trombonists did in fact change to the valve system when it was introduced, but soon changed back to the slide. The only alterations that can be said to have been made to the instrument over the centuries are in the configuration of the mouthpiece, from conical to cup-like, and in an improvement in the slide mechanism by the use of different

metals less affected by friction. Some models have spring buffers to take the shock when the slide is returned smartly to the closed position. Today trombones are made to three different bore specifications: narrow for the French, medium for the English and wide for Americans and Germans.

Technique

Of beautiful constructional and acoustical simplicity, the trombone is the ideal instrument for demonstrating the laws of harmonic progression. The slide has seven different positions, the distance between them diminishing progressively towards the closed position. Each position produces a different set of seven harmonics and thereby a complete range of chromatic notes throughout the compass. Pitch can be refined by lip control and slight adjustments of the slide. Since the slide has to be moved for almost every new note, every note has to be articulated and legato is barely possible. Glissandi are easy, but only over the interval of an augmented fourth. A limited number of shakes

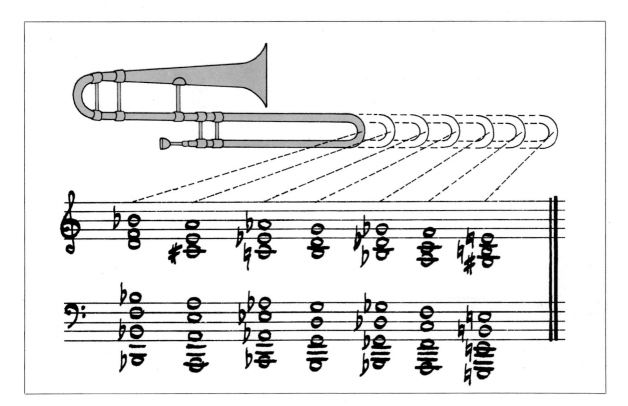

ABOVE
*The trombone's slide positions,
showing how they relate to the scale.
A good trombonist will be able to
sound all these notes, but they
represent the extended range rather
than the working range of the
instrument*

or trills are also possible and the fluctuations of pitch sometimes called for are produced by lip control.

The first trombonist in an orchestra will usually play the ordinary B flat or tenor instrument. The second trombone, however, will often play a tenor with two rotary valves, giving him a choice of B flat, E or F. Using a valve changes the slide positions, but with two valves and the first three positions (together with his all-important 'lip') the trombonist can play just about the whole of the repertoire of the instrument.

The bass trombone is nowadays made in the same pitch as the tenor instrument, but with a larger bore as well as the two rotary valves, giving its lower notes that special bass authority. The musician buying a trombone, by the way, can optionally have the third valve in a different key if he likes, for an instrument of different flexibility.

A contrabass trombone, for which Wagner and Mahler wrote, is a very heavy instrument, described by one trombonist as a 'tank.' It is essentially a slide tuba, and although it is still manufactured by at least one firm (in the U.S.), it is rarely seen, and in British orchestras its music is usually played on a tuba.

Repertoire

The trombone was somewhat neglected after its period of comparative importance in the 16th and 17th centuries when it was appreciated as a status symbol, as well as a sympathetic supporter of singing (around 1685 a collection of Lutheran hymns was published for choir and five trombones). It was not until the time of Berlioz and Wagner that it

a piena voce

retrieved some of what Berlioz described as its 'epic' character. Before that there were occasional passages in operas – the statue scene from Mozart's *Don Giovanni* for example – and oratorio. As the symphony orchestra developed the trombone was slow to be accepted as a regular member. Celebrated symphonies by Mozart and Haydn do not include it at all. Beethoven used it sparingly, but to spectacular effect, in his Fifth Symphony, for example. Beethoven also wrote three *Funeral Equali* or short quartets for trombones, and two of these were played at his funeral. Weber included it in his overture to *Der Freischütz*, blowing something like a small raspberry, and in Schubert's 'Great' C major symphony three trombones play an important role throughout. Rossini is of particular interest because he wrote bravura passages in his operas for the valve trombone which are all but unplayable on the slide.

From the end of the 19th century all the great symphonists scored for three trombones and it is rare indeed, even in the most extravagant scores, that this number is exceeded; and when it is, as in Mahler's Eighth Symphony and Richard Strauss's *Alpine Symphony*, the additional trombones are played off stage.

Among the best known themes in music is that of Wagner's *Tannhauser* overture; this is declared separately by both tenor and bass trombones.

This recitative for trombone occurs in Rimsky–Korsakov's Russian Easter Overture, and expresses the timeless atmosphere of the Russian Orthodox ritual

FAR LEFT
The trombone section of the Chicago Symphony Orchestra

Trombone repertoire

Mozart: *Don Giovanni* (the statue scene)
Beethoven: Symphony No. 5
Weber: Overture, *Der Freischütz*
Schubert: Symphony No. 9 ('Great')
Wagner: Overture, *Tannhauser*

The
Tuba

The part for the tuba is written on the bass clef, under the stave carrying the part for the trombone. The tuba is not a transposing instrument, but should the part for the bass tuba go very low the sign 8va is used, obviating ledger lines and indicating that the music is to sound an octave lower than written.

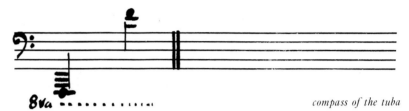

compass of the tuba

ABOVE
Not surprisingly, the identity of the tuba player in this picture is difficult to confirm

A cuddly-looking instrument, clutched like an overgrown teddy bear, the bell directed at an oblique angle and flaring outwards above the head of the player, the tuba has been described as a plumber's nightmare. This is on account of the labyrinth of conical tubing, different lengths of which are opened and closed by a number of piston or rotary valves. The longer the length of tube opened up by the valves, the longer the air column that has to be set vibrating by the player, using a large, deep cup mouthpiece. Thus low notes take longer to speak or sound than high ones. Tubas are the lowest sounding of the brass instruments and they are to the brass section what the double bass is to the string section, their role being mainly to give support to the lower sounding brass.

History

The name referred originally to the Roman war horn. The history of the tuba is a short one, but the multiplicity of types and names is such that even the *Oxford Companion to Music* admits that to define 'tuba' is impossible.

Those who seek clarification will discover that some tubas are held inclined to the left shoulder and some to the right. Moreover some drawings and photographs display the instrument lying horizontal, others plonked disgracefully upside down. There are, or have been, 9-foot, 12-foot, 14-foot and 16-foot tubas and one called the BBB flat contrabass standing nine feet high with some 36 feet of tubing, a nightmare for several plumbers.

What provoked the development of this unruly tribe of low-pitched brass instruments was the invention of the valve in the early 19th century.

Large keyed bugle horns, a crossbreed between horns and trumpets, were difficult to play well and had a number of weak and out-of-tune notes; this was due partly to the wide spacing and large

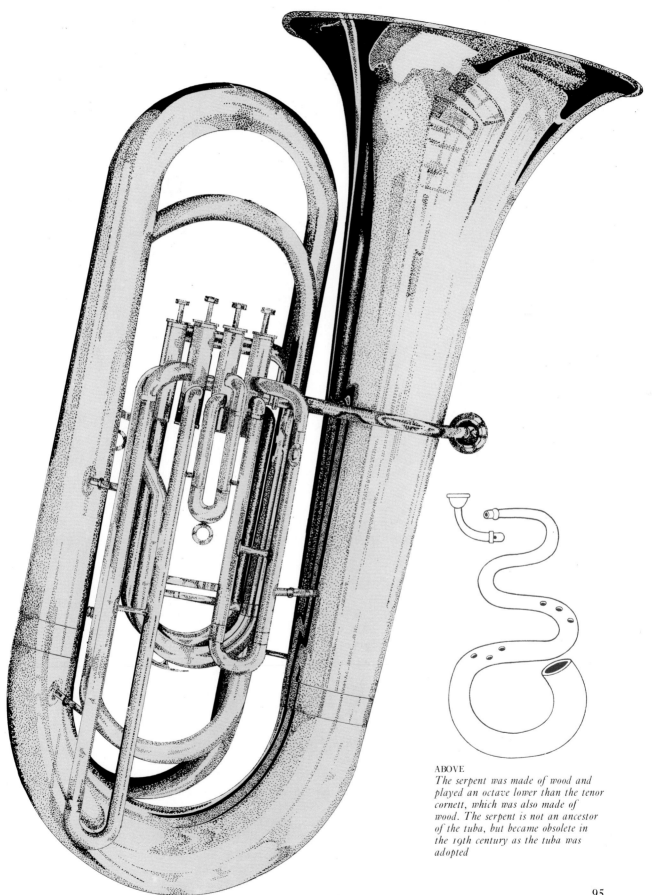

ABOVE
The serpent was made of wood and played an octave lower than the tenor cornett, which was also made of wood. The serpent is not an ancestor of the tuba, but became obsolete in the 19th century as the tuba was adopted

THE EUPHONIUM.

The euphonium is a tenor tuba which was common in marching bands, especially in the days before bandleaders such as Sousa began designing their own bass brass instruments

RIGHT
This mammoth tuba, with 34 feet of tubing, was brought to England from America in 1907. Unbelievably, it was lost or mislaid in the basement of Paxman, the London instrument makers, until 1957, when this picture was taken

diameter of the key holes in the long tube. Once the valve was invented it was possible to fold that long tubing neatly and scientifically, to bore it with holes of equal diameter and to fit them with hermetically sealing valves. While composers complained that the application of valves to the French horn, the trumpet and in particular the trombone impaired the characteristic timbre, in this case there were no real comparisons to be made and they were glad to have this new, lowest-of-all sounding instrument that would gradually replace the ophicleide (a large form of keyed bugle) and the serpent (also keyed, its length compressed by a series of wriggles).

Tubas in various sizes were made from about 1835 onwards to a specification of trombonist Wilhelm Wieprecht, bandmaster of the Prussian Dragoon Guards, but it was not until late in the century that they were to be seen and heard in the orchestra. Then, as indeed now, their most common use was in military and brass bands, where they assumed a number of different shapes. Probably the best-known 'special' variety is the Sousaphone, which is built to the specification of John Philip Sousa in circular form with the huge bell facing forwards.

In orchestral music oval-shaped tubas called Wagner Tuben are sometimes used. These use a horn mouthpiece, and were developed by the Bohemian firm of instrument makers called Cerveny, and then re-invented some thirty years later by Wagner, who wanted a timbre somewhere between that of a true tuba and a horn in the operatic cycle *Der Ring des Nibelungen*. The Wagner Tuben have been scored for by other composers since Wagner, including Bruckner and Stravinsky. The usual tubas to be seen in the orchestra are the tenor and/or bass.

Technique

The whole range of tonguing from single to agile triple and flutter are used, but the amount of air needed to sound the tuba restricts the length of legato passages, particularly those in the lower register. The lowest register is played with a very slack lip and relaxed and dropped lower jaw. The technique is basically the same as that for other brass instruments with valves.

Repertoire

For a new instrument with limited powers of expression the tuba's repertoire is far from dull. 'The tuba is precious,' wrote Rimsky-Korsakov, 'on account of the strength and beauty of its low notes. Thanks to the valves it has sufficient mobility.' Rimsky-Korsakov first introduced double tonguing in his *Schéhérazade* and several composers since then, including Honnegger and Shostakovitch, have written passages for flutter tonguing. Mahler included tuba glissandi in his scores, and a well known passage in Wagner's prelude to *Die Meistersinger* ends in a trill. The muted tuba can be heard in the Mussorgsky-Ravel *Pictures at an Exhibition*, including an outstanding unmuted solo in the 'Bydlo' section of that piece. The opening bars of Mussorgsky's *Night on the Bare Mountain* include the tuba.

Rimsky-Korsakov holds the view of some musicians that Brahms was not a good orchestrator. Brahms (1833–97) was a younger man than Wagner (1813–83) and was overshadowed by him; his writing for the tuba was more restrained than that of Wagner, but the way in which he wrote for it, not only to buttress fortissimo passages but in particular to execute series of wide leaps, as in the Second Symphony, was in fact more advanced than that of other composers of his time. Gustav Holst used a euphonium (tenor tuba) in the 'Mars' section of *The Planets*. The repertoire for solo tuba could be said to have culminated in the Tuba Concerto by Ralph Vaughan Williams.

One of Mussorgsky's *Pictures* is 'Bydlo', a drawing of a peasant's ox-cart. It begins quietly, as though the ox-cart is moving toward the listener, generates a quite relentless drama, and then moves away down the road. The solo tuba plays the lumbering theme

Tuba repertoire

Rimsky–Korsakov: *Schéhérazade*
Wagner: Overture, *Die Meistersinger*
Mussorgsky–Ravel: 'Bydlo' from *Pictures at an Exhibition*
Mussorgsky: *Night on the Bare Mountain*
Brahms: Symphony No. 3
Vaughan Williams: Tuba Concerto
Holst: 'Mars' from *The Planets*

THE
PERCUSSION
INSTRUMENTS

The Timpani

compass of the timpani

The part for the timpani, or kettle drums, is written on a stave above that of the first stringed instrument, be it harp, violins, or that other percussion instrument, the piano. The notes to which the two or three drums are to be tuned are named at the beginning of the score, any alterations being indicated as they occur. Each drum has a compass of a fifth.

The art of the timpanist is infinitely more complex and subtle than would at first appear. There never have been infant prodigies and most master drummers are middle-aged, with a great depth of orchestral playing experience that gives them the authority and sensitivity essential to their successful contribution to the music.

The timpanist can spend as much time tuning as playing. He will arrive early on the platform and can be observed bending low over each of the metal kettles mounted on wheeled frames, tapping the skin and adjusting the tuning. There are two methods of tuning: one is by means of a number of T-handles around the rim, the other is by means of a foot pedal. The latter is for what is called the pedal or chromatic drum. The timpanist will be equipped with at least four different types of beaters or drum sticks ranging from soft to hard; the choice will be dictated by the score. Different beaters produce different sounds but so also do the points at which the drum head is struck. It is worth focussing attention on the timpanist throughout a concert in order to understand the nature of his responsibilities.

History

The correct English name for the bowl-shaped drums is kettle, but the word timpani is used in scores. The word timpani derives from a Greek word that means to strike, and this word was itself imported into Greece from Turkey where it referred to a drum used in orgiastic ceremonies connected with the worship of the earth mother Cybele.

European kettle drums have an honourable and a fairly well-defined history, at least as far back as the 13th century when the Crusaders took a great fancy to the *naqqarya*, the bowl-shaped drums they saw mounted on the camels and horses of their Islamic adversaries. From the Middle East the naqqarya were then carried into and across Europe and a small version reached England by the end of the century; they were then called *nakers*.

In Islam before the 13th century where the drums were already an established symbol of grandeur and power for both military and peaceful occasions, they were often played in groups of hundreds, accompanied by hundreds of trumpets. This extravagant prestige did not immediately follow them to England. The merry and despised bands of wandering minstrels of the middle ages, ever out for the latest and greatest in gossip and music, adopted the nakers to accompany

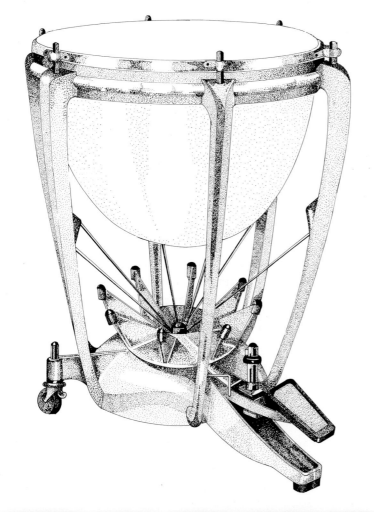

Timpanist Andrew Smith of the Philharmonia tuning the pedal or chromatic drum

Nakers slung from the waist. This detail is from a 14th century Italian manuscript

A woodcut from 1584 by Jost Ammon, showing mounted kettle drums

their own rumbustious forms of entertainment, as many an illuminated work of the period shows. In these illustrations the nakers are beaten with knobbed or curved sticks. Sometimes they are played on the ground, sometimes slung about the waist. In restoration performances of early music in this century the latter position has led to them being called knickers. (Future historians as well as American readers may find this musical joke confusing: 'knickers' is British slang for underpants, and sends school children into paroxysms of sniggers.)

The larger naqqarya have a more dignified history, having been introduced straight into polite society in 1542 by Henry VIII who ordered them, with the personnel to play them, from Vienna where they were already popular. Their prestige never faltered from that time and can be seen to be retained today at, for example, Trooping the Colour when the caparisoned drum horse leads the Household Cavalry in advance of the British Monarch.

By the end of the 16th century these large drums were called kettle drums, and were already used dismounted and placed on stands. They were first introduced into the orchestra by that arch-intriguer of the court of Louis XIV, Lully, who was in charge of the military music. Then, and for a period after, their principal role was to provide dramatic emphasis and extra volume.

In a way, pictorial evidence from 16th century Islam leads to the next stage in the use of the drum as well as the particular use of a number of other exotic percussion instruments. One painting of 1561 shows an orchestra of several pairs of fixed drums in the company of trumpets, castanets, cymbals and tambourines. This particular ensemble provided music for a wedding celebration. Another painting of 1592 shows a Turkish military band with twelve pairs of bowl-shaped drums accompanying rows of trumpets and shawms (precursors of the oboe). These types of ensembles were similar to those of the Janissaries, the infantry of the Ottoman Turks, and these had been heard on the further-flung frontiers of Europe and inspired the popular fashion for what was called Turkish music. This craze lasted well into the 19th century, when even pianos were furnished with an extra number of pedals which banged drums and bells and produced a reedy string tone in imitation of the shawms. Mozart, Haydn and Beethoven were all responsible for composing quasi-Turkish music with its characteristically strong beat.

In England Purcell is believed to have been the first to use the kettle drums, in *The Fairy Queen* (1687). From this time and a good while afterwards the timpani were tuned in fifths. The limitation of their use in the orchestra was caused by limitations of tuning; only when these were overcome could more interesting music be composed for them.

The problems facing drum makers were manifold, even though the instrument consists of no more than a skin stretched over a bowl. The shape and dimensions of the bowl or shell in relation to the drum head are important, as is the choice and preparation of the skin. The best skins are taken from well-fed calves of not more than twelve months old. After the process of removing the hair and treating them with salt to preserve them, they are stretched. A stretched skin is then lapped over a hoop that resembles an embroidery frame, so that the spine of the animal is visibly dead centre (if the term may be forgiven). The strongest part of the animal's skin is around the neck, and for the best results the striking spot is a few inches or so to the right or the left of the neck. The depth and shape of the shell in relation to the diameter of the drum-head should be such that the sound waves transmitted into it when the head is struck should follow a path with the minimum number of deflections. This will produce a clean sound with the right harmonics present at the right strength, the fifth and the fourth being important. A hole in the bottom of the shell ensures that the concussed air within the bowl has an escape and does not split the skin. Incidentally, for some reason not perfectly understood, the kettle drum does not sound its fundamental but the first harmonic, the octave.

Various methods of tuning were devised over the years, but the T-handle and pedal techniques are the only ones that have survived. When the pedal drum was devised it was hailed as a great new invention, but this was not quite true: in both India and Africa chromatic drums with a remarkably wide compass had already been played with considerable virtuosity for hundreds of years. With these drums the tension on the skin is finely controlled by thongs and braces stretched and slackened by hand or arm pressure. Open-ended drums were tuned by holding them over a fire and others by a blob of rice paste plastered in the middle of the head.

A common complaint about the modern pedal drums is that the assembly of rods beneath the shell impairs the resonance. Few members of an audience would notice this, but many notice when synthetic heads are used, as they often are nowadays. These have a dull white appearance – unlike the somewhat transparent and grained look of the natural skin – and the sound is lacking in upper harmonics. Plastic heads are becoming common because they are weatherproof.

In early cultures drums have been held sacred and been connected with magic and power. Among many tribes drums were hidden when not in use and the sight of them by alien eyes, in particular those of women, was considered a serious offence, while their destruction has always been connected with disarray and doom. The drums are the one instrument of the orchestra whose sonorous and sometimes thunderous voice has never been compared with that of the mortal human but always with that of the immortal gods.

ABOVE KETTLE-DRUMS.
The shape of the kettle drum shell has undergone many changes. These shallow ones are characteristic of the early 19th century

Technique

Beethoven's Violin Concerto begins with four simple, solo drum beats. 'When you can play this, you will be a good timpanist,' said a celebrated conductor to an eminent orchestral musician. And he was right. Those simple-sounding Ds must be struck at the right spot on the skin, at a certain distance to the side of the neck of the calf. And that skin must be in tune with a good harmonic fifth audible not just where it is struck but at six to eight points round the circumference of the drum head.

A steady sense of rhythm is of course essential to any percussionist, but so is a very good ear. The timpanist may have to tune up and down several times in the course of a work, often with the orchestra playing

along in a key unrelated to the one he is preparing for. There is no need for the timpanist to indulge in exaggerated gestures when he plays, flinging his arms above his head in the mode of drum majorettes. Everything depends on good wrist work. For *piano* the drum is struck nearest the rim, with shallow strokes; for *forte*, in the usual position with deeper strokes. Over fifty types of sticks or beaters have been specified, and these range from a knife blade to a wire brush. Different positions of striking are also called for – near the rim, on the rim and, very rarely, in the middle of the head. There are also different methods of damping with the fingers or with a cloth.

Since drum-heads of skin are sensitive to alterations in atmospheric pressure, the timpanist has to be ever-vigilant over his tuning. And kettle drums are easily excited by sounds going on about them and are apt to start 'singing' without being asked; damping cloths or pads are used to keep them quiet. After a concert the drum heads will be slackened and wooden covers placed over them for protection.

Repertoire

Beethoven was the first composer to use the kettle drums as solo instruments. The opening of his Violin Concerto has been mentioned, but in the Scherzo of his Ninth Symphony he introduced what was then considered to be a revolutionary effect: drums tuned in octaves. When Bliss introduced drums tuned to sevenths in his 'Pastoral' the effect passed unnoticed.

Mozart and Haydn did not make much use of kettle drums, and when they did it was mainly for support in loud passages. Mention has also been made of Turkish music and there are echoes of this in Haydn's 'Military' Symphony in the percussion section.

In the 19th century when the normal complement of drums was three and the pedal had been developed composers seized upon this new resource with cunning and eagerness, and by the early 20th century Sibelius, Mahler, Ravel, Bartók and Strauss seemed to have exploited every trick and stick in the trade. 'After hearing the operas *Salome* and *Rosenkavalier* I am convinced,' wrote the timpanist Henry Taylor, 'that Strauss has reached the limit in safe and effective scoring for the pedal timpani.' There is no doubt however that for spectacular musical thrills nothing can compare with the sixteen kettle drums hammered by ten drummers in the *Tuba Mirum* section of the Berlioz *Requiem*.

Timpani repertoire

Beethoven: Violin Concerto
Beethoven: Symphony No. 9
Bartók: *Sonata for Two Pianos
and Percussion*
Berlioz: *Tuba Mirum* from the
Requiem
Carter: Piano Concerto

Percussion

The staves for the percussion instruments are massed in the middle of the score. Who plays what depends on manpower, availability and ability.

The *glockenspiel* and *celesta* are both *metallophones*, the first having a resemblance to a small xylophone and the second to a small piano.

'Glockenspiel' means 'bell-play' in German. The glockenspiel used in marching bands is a set of steel bars set in a lyre-shaped frame. Mozart specified an *instrumento d'acciaio* (steel instrument) for the part of Papageno's magic bells in *Die Zauberflöte*; this may have been a set of small tuned bells played from a keyboard like a modern celesta. These bells were also used by carillon players for practice. The modern orchestral glockenspiel has two rows of steel bars covering $2\frac{1}{2}$ octaves, and is played with beaters or mallets with hard or soft heads. The sound is small and bright and was used by Tchaikovsky in the 'Chinese Dance' in his *Nutcracker* ballet.

While the glockenspiel is played by a percussionist, the celesta is often played by a pianist. It was invented in 1886 by Mustel, the maker

compass of the glockenspiel

FAR LEFT
Modern orchestral timpani, or pedal drums

BELOW
The percussion section of the London Symphony Orchestra. From bongos to xylophone, there are about sixteen instruments in all. Some of the drums are half hidden and the Chinese blocks on a stand in front of the large gong are barely visible

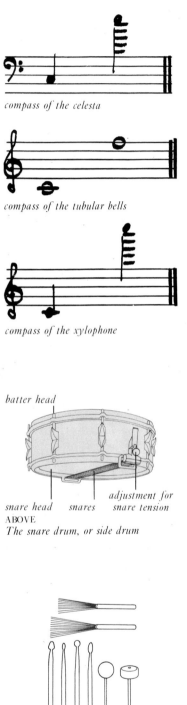

compass of the celesta

compass of the tubular bells

compass of the xylophone

batter head

snare head   snares   adjustment for
                        snare tension
ABOVE
The snare drum, or side drum

ABOVE
*A selection of beaters, sticks and wire
brushes used by percussionists*

of harmoniums. Its series of steel plates are attached to wood resonators, which have dampers controlled by a pedal. The compass varies from four to five octaves of heavenly tinkles, much favoured by orchestral colourists from the late 19th century onwards. Tchaikovsky first used it in the 'Dance of the Sugar-plum Fairy' in the *Nutcracker*. Ravel scored for it; Bartók wrote *Music for Strings, Percussion and Celesta*.

The *chimes*, or *tubular bells*, are also made of metal. They cover a chromatic compass of an octave and a third. The eighteen bells are hung in two rows and are struck near the top. 'Their effect is dramatic rather than musical,' was the opinion of Berlioz. Rimsky-Korsakov said that there are no ugly timbres in the orchestra, but the bells are written for with some restraint, the confusion of overtones in their timbre making them sound, to some ears at least, uneasily out of tune. Sooner or later any book on instruments of the orchestra must mention Tchaikovsky's *1812 Overture*. Now is the moment. The chimes sound out in this overture, imitating the jubilant bell towers of Moscow, drowned out only by the firing of cannon; sometimes in open air performances, real artillery cannon are used!

The xylophone (*xylo* is Greek for wood) is of ancient Asiatic bars, played with beaters similar to those used for the glockenspiel. The resonance of the bars is augmented by metal tubes fixed below each one. The whole arrangement, which when seen from above resembles an outsize piano keyboard, is built into a wheeled frame supplied with brakes to prevent it wandering around the platform.

The xylophone (*xylo* is Greek for wood) is of ancient Asiatic origin, its highest development being reached in Java in the 14th century. It has always been a popular instrument in many areas of Africa where often huge groups of different-sized xylophones play complex polyrhythmic and polyphonic music. The xylophone was depicted by Praetorius and Mersenne. It was made popular in Europe by a Russian, Guslov, who gave recitals on it. In the middle of the 19th century the xylophone was absorbed into the symphony orchestra, being first used by Saint-Saëns in his 'Danse Macabre' (1874) to describe the rattling of bones. The third movement of Bartók's *Music for Strings, Percussion and Celesta* begins with a xylophone solo.

Percussion of indefinite pitch

Of the three drums in this section of the orchestra the *snare drum* is both the most difficult to play and the most familiar. It is also called side drum, because it is slung and worn to one side in military, fife, pipe and other marching bands. The shallow metal shell is supported on a stand in the orchestra, at a slight angle for ease of playing. The slim sticks, made of hickory or lancewood, are slightly tapered towards the tip. The two vellums are made of a calf skin, the top one called the batter head and the bottom the snare head. The snares are eight to ten gut or wire strings stretched under the lower head; these vibrate when the batter head is struck, producing a brilliant rattling sound. The snares can be slackened off, or dampened by placing a handkerchief under them, to produce a muted sound.

The snare drummer has a special language for particular beats and rhythmic ornamentation. The rim shot, a dry, explosive sound, is produced not by striking the rim but by laying one stick across the rim with the tip on the batter head and striking it with the other. 'Flam, drag and paradiddle' can only be described in notation.

'Mammy-daddy' is another name for a double beat on alternate hands. This is the basis of the long, continuous close roll such as can be heard at the beginning of Rossini's overture to *The Silken Ladder*. One of the most impressive of all side drum parts is in Ravel's Boléro, in which it keeps up a short insistent rhythm throughout. Carl Nielsen's Fifth Symphony also has an extensive and impressive snare drum part.

The snare drum replaced the tenor or military drum, which has a deeper shell, no snares and is as a rule played with soft sticks. The sound is consequently dull and although it can be used for accentuation and colour, it is never given interesting or outstanding parts to play.

The *bass drum* stands vertically, the rim of the shallow wooden shell facing the audience. This was originally known as the Turkish drum. Sometimes it has two heads, sometimes only one, the former model producing somewhat greater clarity. It is beaten with upward – or downward – glancing blows with a soft stick, and sometimes brushed simultaneously on the other side with a switch of sorts. When the craze for Turkish music came about in the 18th century it lasted for about forty years, and during this period the bass drum gained in popularity and was used by Haydn in his 'Military' Symphony and by Beethoven, who clearly had a penchant for oriental exotica, in the Finale of his Ninth Symphony. The deep voice of the bass drum is often described as being felt rather than heard. Sometimes it carries an attachment that enables a single cymbal to be mounted on top.

The *tambourine*, the last of the orchestral instruments to have a vellum stretched over a hoop, is of the greatest antiquity, going back to the third millennium at least. It is generally associated with the dance and in Near and Middle-Eastern societies was once the only instrument that women were permitted to play. In the Royal Palace in Siena there is a fascinating fresco by Lorenzetti depicting the performance, by women, of an extremely formal and restrained serpentine dance to the sole accompaniment of a female singer with tambourine; this suggests that, for some reason that we can no longer trace, the instrument may have had some connection with goddesses or the earth mother. The tambourine was introduced into the orchestra during the boom in Turkish music and is mostly used to evoke dancing of a more abandoned nature than that seen in the fresco. The sound is produced by striking it with the fingers, the knuckles or the palm of the hand, or by shaking it; in every case the little metal discs in the rim of the shallow wooden shell are shaken into life, as they are if a moistened finger or thumb is passed over the vellum.

This is an example of notation for the side drum, or snare drum. In this case the beat is that called 'stroke, flam and drag, paradiddle'

LEFT
This is the famous two-bar phrase which is played by the side-drummer 165 times in Ravel's Boléro, which is 332 bars long, and takes about thirteen minutes to play. The side drummer plays throughout the entire piece, except for the last two bars, and has to play a relentless crescendo, beginning very softly and joined by a second drummer at bar 291. The whole piece, but especially the side drum part, is an exercise in dynamic control

ABOVE
The orchestral bass drum on a stand

ABOVE
The castanets. This is a drawing of the original Spanish type for which there is really no substitute. One piece which features several percussion instruments, including the castanets, is Rimsky-Korsakov's Cappriccio Espagnol

The *castanets* were also used for dancing from earliest times, although originally they were probably flatter, clapper-type instruments unlike the shell-shaped, hollowed-out castanets known today, which are often played with considerable virtuosity, at least by the Spaniards. Spanish dancers generally play them in pairs, one of higher pitch than the other and called the female, the other lower pitched and called the male. In the orchestra this distinction has been lost. Moreover, instead of the castanets being looped over the thumb, two shells are attached to a handle and played rather in the manner of the London street 'spoon bashers,' rapped on the hands or knees rather than clacked with supple fingers. The sound of the castanets has therefore become one of the most disappointing in the orchestra, usually trying unsuccessfully to recreate the excitement of those Spanish dances.

Yet two more instruments of the percussion section came into the 18th century orchestra by way of the Turkish bands: the *cymbal* and the *triangle*.

Cymbals are known to go back to the second millennium BC when one of their functions was to accompany wrestling. But smaller cymbals, called *crotales* in orchestral scores, are also of considerable antiquity and were used to keep time during the dance. Cymbals are not of Turkish origin but the best ones used today come from Turkey, or from China. These are made to a jealously guarded formula consisting of a proportion of copper to a smaller proportion of tin. The large cymbals measure about 14 inches across and they have a central boss or raised portion through which a holding strap is passed. After they are clashed, they are held high for all to see and marvel at, as well as to allow the reverberations to spill out unimpeded. They are damped by pressing them inwards rapidly against the chest. Sometimes they are struck with a stick, and occasionally rubbed together to give a curious metallic shuffling sound. They were first used in an operatic score of 1680, and then forgotten until the 18th century when all schools of composers took advantage of the penetrating timbre produced by the enharmonic partials in the sound. 'They ally themselves,' wrote Berlioz, 'incomparably well . . . with sentiments of extreme ferocity . . . or with feverish excitements of a bacchanalian orgy' – a description which would have shocked those Victorian ladies who treadled away at the Turkish pedal effects on their expensive drawing room pianofortes.

Rimsky-Korsakov rejects Berlioz's admiration for Gluck as an orchestrator, preferring to name Weber and Mendelssohn as the first colourists. But the first orchestrators were often seeking effects rather than colours and this is partly why so many innovations were introduced into operatic rather than symphonic music. Thus the triangle was first used by Gluck in *Iphigénie en Tauride* in 1779 and only thereafter was it heard in symphonic works, 'Anitra's Dance' in the *Peer Gynt* suite by Grieg being an example. As with the cymbal, the penetrating timbre of the triangle is due to the enharmonic partials in the sound. Single notes are struck on the outside of the steel triangle and tremolos from side to side within the frame. As those who have attended performances of Leopold Mozart's 'Toy Symphony' performed by amateurs will know, this apparently simple instrument can give a feeble or ignorant player moments of great humiliation, particularly if it decides to swing away when the beater is poised to strike.

The last instrument in this section is the *tam-tam*, a shallow, suspended bronze gong with a long, colourful reverberation. Tam-tams are often objects of art as much as musical instruments and it is generally the orchestra rather than the percussionist who possesses one. Although members of the audience are certainly not welcome climbing all over the platform before a concert starts, there are sometimes opportunities at the end to approach the platform and peer closely at the instruments of the percussion section before they are wrapped up, dismantled or bundled away. The tam-tam is worth examining not only to determine its country of origin but to see if it is engraved. The large, flat tam-tam with a shallow rim will be from China, and that with a deeper rim will come from Burma. Those engraved with a dragon are the most precious. Nowadays, according to James Holland, percussionists differentiate between the tam-tam, with an indefinite pitch, and the gong, with a definite pitch.

A work that includes all the instruments mentioned in this whole section on percussion is Ravel's *Daphnis and Chloë*. Some of the late symphonies of Shostakovitch, and Tippett's Third Symphony, use many of them as well.

ABOVE
A Boosey and Hawkes triangle, with holder and beater

Percussion repertoire

Mozart: *Die Zauberflöte*
Tchaikovsky: 'Chinese Dance' and 'Dance of the Sugar-Plum Fairy' from the *Nutcracker*
Tchaikovsky: *1812 Overture*
Saint–Saëns: *Danse Macabre*
Bartók: *Music for Strings, Percussion and Celesta*
Rimsky–Korsakov: *Capriccio Espagnol*
Rossini: Overture, *La Scala di Seta*
Nielson: Symphony No. 5
Haydn: Symphony No. 100 ('Military')
Grieg: *Peer Gynt* suite no. 1
Mozart (Leopold): *Cassation for Orchestra and Toys* ('Toy Symphony')
Ravel: *Daphnis and Chloë*
Tippett: Symphony No. 3
Shostakovitch: Symphony No. 15

This is the percussion part from the last page of Haydn's 'Military' Symphony, a big hit when first played in London late in the 18th century. Timpani, triangle, cymbals and bass drum are all crashing away to provide a 'Turkish' flavour

THE KEYBOARD INSTRUMENTS

The Organ

The organ is the earliest known of all mechanically operated musical instruments and not, as is sometimes stated, one of the earliest musical instruments. The first known organ dates from the 3rd century BC. This was a *hydraulos*, with a clever system of maintaining wind pressure by incorporating a water cistern in the wind reservoir; when the wind pressure sank, the water level rose to maintain it.

The story of two thousand years of development, from the small hydraulos to mammoth instruments with thousands of pipes, a multitude of timbres and inbuilt gale force winds, cannot be encompassed in anything less than a major work in several volumes. In almost every century and every country the construction and timbres of the organ were enriched by a process of evolution which was exploited by both composers and performers. As early as the 14th century the organ was called the King of instruments, and in the late 19th century was described as 'the most perfect musical instrument that the ingenuity of man has hitherto devised.'

Until the 18th century the organ had been a major instrument for the expression of polyphonic music, which required a transparent texture so that separate parts could be clearly heard. Many churches in Britain and Europe still possess small 18th century organs with voices of silvery sweetness which are perfect for music of many strands, and a considerable number of larger organs of that period also still survive and are treasured for the information they provide about construction in their time, as well as the authentic timbre of contemporaneous music. Automatic or barrel organs were also popular in the 18th century and these were skilfully constructed by some of the greatest organ builders. Barrel organs consist of a barrel turned by hand which bristles with pins; when the barrel is turned each pin makes a pipe speak. The pinning of barrels was done in such a manner that the tunes, their harmonies and the ornamentation were accurately consistent with the style of the period when, in many cases, churches preferred a barrel organ to some fumbling part-time human organist. A book published in 1775, and recently republished in facsimile, called *La Tonotéchnie ou l' Art de Noter les Cylindres*, by Father Joseph Engramelle, describes the detailed care given to the pinning of barrels and the method used to ensure the correct tempo of the music. The music of a barrel organ is therefore among the most valuable sources of information about the authentic performance of hymns and popular music of the time.

Many large organs built in the 20th century incorporate features from early instruments, so that organists have at their disposal the timbres suitable for an historically wide range of music.

In the middle of the 18th century, when the piano began to replace the harpsichord, the symphony orchestra began to replace the

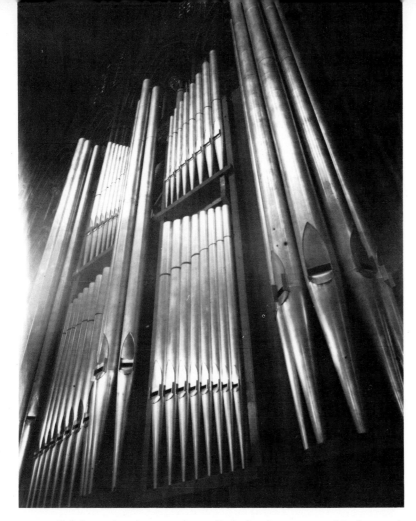

LEFT
The organ in Westminster Abbey played for the first time at the coronation of George VI in 1936

organ. Celebrated composers wrote little for the organ at this time and, in the case at least of Beethoven and Mozart, only in their youth. In the 19th century the volume that some organs could produce was equal to, and sometimes greater than, that of the orchestra, and could drown it. Major composers preferred over a hundred musicians to over a hundred stops, and when they combined organ and orchestra they were inclined to use the former going full blast or, to use the correct technical term, full organ. (Organ stop terminology is a language of its own, and a simple list of terms commonly met with can fill several pages.)

Holst in *The Planets*, Mahler in two of his symphonies, Saint-Saëns, Richard Strauss and Respighi have all included the organ in orchestral scores, making the interesting assumption that the halls in which the works were to be performed would be furnished with an organ – which all the new ones of the affluent late Victorian period were. And if composers did not wholeheartedly agree with Berlioz, who wrote that orchestra and organ together produced a 'detestable effect,' they none the less scored for it sparingly. The effectiveness of the organ from the point of view of the audience is not so much the sound itself nor the physical impact of the sound (it can set the seats and those sitting in them a-tremble) but the fact that all the sound comes from a different position in the hall, from above the orchestra, adding another spatial dimension to the music. Copland's Symphony for Organ and Orchestra (1924) is among the most recent orchestral works to include the organ.

Organ repertoire

Holst: *The Planets*
Mahler: Symphony No. 2 ('Resurrection')
Saint-Saëns: Symphony No. 3
Strauss: *Also sprach Zarathustra*
Copland: Symphony for Organ and Orchestra
Haydn: Organ Concerto No. 1

The Harpsichord

The harpsichord has a shallower cabinet than that of the piano, and the legs are prettier. If historical accuracy has been observed in its making it will have no foot pedals but instead hand stops placed in the right and the left of the keyboard. Very likely there will be two manuals or keyboards which are stepped. Harpsichordists sit very still as they play. As the strings are plucked by means of tiny quills, no additional volume is to be gained by exerting force or using arm weight. Only a rapid, almost plucking action of the fingers is necessary. No changes of volume are possible, but alterations of timbre are, and these are achieved by a combination of the hand stops. The hand stops engage additional ranks of strings, or alter the point at which they are plucked. The number of ranks of strings and hand stops vary according to the date and make of the instrument.

The role of the harpsichord in the small 17th and 18th century ensembles was that of support and accompaniment. This is called *continuo* playing and it can involve extemporization. The most musical, authentic, effective or correct manner of playing the continuo and extemporizations has provoked countless treatises, books, articles, lectures and comment since its beginning. In the end all the problems have been very satisfactorily resolved and the battles quelled by the use of one short sentence: it is all a question of taste. In 1717 in his *L'Art de Toucher le Clavecin* François Couperin frequently uses the word *goust* (*goût* means taste) to explain what he means more clearly. Francesco Geminiani (1687–1762), who was accompanied by Handel, wrote *Rules for Playing in True Taste*. And writers in this century who are engaged in the pursuit of knowledge about early music will often guide their readers by calling upon their feeling for good taste.

Early music for harpsichord continuo was not written out in great detail; thus ornamentation, tempi, registration (i.e. choice of stops) were all matters of taste and style of the period. When, from the middle of the 19th century until the 1950s, the harpsichord was written off as obsolete, having been driven out of favour by the piano, the whole tradition of harpsichord playing was lost. Its sound was described as that of a bird cage thrashed with a toasting fork, and all 17th and 18th century music was played on the piano. The taste of the time heard nothing wrong in performing the continuo on the piano or leaving it out altogether. But in the 1950s, on account of a well-rooted and growing curiosity among musicologists, craftsmen, private collectors and museums, the harpsichord was reinstated as an instrument for which, in early music, there is no substitute. A great deal of restoration of neglected instruments ensued and an increasing number of books were written about the harpsichord, its history and technique, and there were reprints, re-translations and facsimile reproductions of earlier manuals of instruction such as Couperin's *L'Art de Toucher*.

ABOVE
A typical 18th century ensemble in a well-to-do household, with violins, viola da gamba, singer and exceptionally long-tailed harpsichord with the lid closed. This social setting was recorded by Chodowiecki, the 'German Hogarth' (see also page 13)

So much research led to the belief that in order to come closest to the heart and the intention of the music it was important to use an instrument of the date and nationality of the composer. To play Couperin on a late 18th century machine of English make is today considered anachronistic. Some scholars criticized Wanda Landowska, the first harpsichordist of international repute, for recording the 48 Preludes and Fugues of J.S. Bach on a modern Pleyel machine with pedals and a 16 foot stop. (But musicianship always triumphs, and those recordings remain examples of illuminating interpretation.)

Today the choice of reproduction harpsichords ranges from the earliest single manual machine, with two ranks of strings, to the larger more elaborate ones with two manuals, three ranks of strings and four or five hand stops.

Plucked keyboard instruments date from at least the late 15th century. It is believed that the harpsichord is a development of the psaltery, which was plucked by the fingers or a quill. How or when the mechanism to pluck from below, by means of keys operating quilled jacks, was invented is not known. Some of the earliest extant instruments are of fine linear elegance and made with exquisite attention to detail and accuracy. A harpsichord in the Victoria and Albert Museum in London by Giovanni Baffo, dated 1574, has a row of jacks that are uniform in thickness to 0.004 of an inch. As with all instruments of this period and later, the Baffo is contained in an outer case; this is a form of insulation against changes of temperature.

In the 17th and 18th centuries Flanders, France and England were each producing quantities of fine instruments. Among the most celebrated makers were Ruckers, Taskin and Kirckman. The last manufactured his instruments from roughly the middle of the 18th century onwards. A number of these have a Venetian swell – a sort of blind over the soundboard, operated by a pedal; when opened the full

BELOW
A study in concentration: Gustav Leonhardt, one of today's most highly regarded harpsichord soloists. The view shows the ranks of strings and the row of jacks lying under the jack rail, a device which prevents them from leaping out of their slots

volume and all the harmonics can be heard, when closed the volume is diminished and a number of the higher harmonics snuffed out. This was introduced in an attempt to compete with the loud and soft of the piano, but some time before the middle of the next century the battle was lost and the piano reigned supreme.

Technique

Harpsichords can have two or three ranks or sets of strings. Two will be at normal 8 foot pitch, like a piano; these can be used singly or together. A third rank of strings will sound an octave above the 8 foot; this is called the 4 foot stop and it adds brilliance to the sound. At the start of a work the harpsichordist chooses the registration or combination of stops he needs. Some harpsichords include buff (a form of muting), lute and harp stops. Too many changes of registration in the course of a work are considered to be in bad taste. Graceful phrasing, clear articulation, and flowing ornamentation that does not impair the forward movement of the music are considered to be the ideal.

Like Bach and his contemporaries, harpsichordists will know how to lay out a scale and to tune to mean tone or equal temperament. They will also know how to requill. The little chips of quill in the jack, which come from the flight feathers of large wild birds such as condors and ravens, can break, drop out or become too soft. All the quills must pluck with equal force.

Finger technique is only part of the skill needed by the harpsichordist. He must be able to read and interpret a figured bass – notes with numbers beside them indicating the harmony. Sometimes there are notes and no numbers. The harmonies have then to be played in the style of the music – plain, ornamented or sometimes echoing phrases from other instruments or singers. The harpsichordist will also be called upon to direct the ensemble so that there is an uniformity of tasteful style at the right tempo. And just as the conductor of the modern orchestra must have a working knowledge of several instruments, so must the harpsichordist know about viols, lutes, keyless flutes, and baroque fiddles and oboes.

Repertoire

'Until the harpsichord lost favour,' wrote Arnold Dolmetsch, 'there were two in each orchestra. At the first sat the concert-master, who accompanied soli; at the second the accompanist who played the tuttis.' And today, in restoration early music, two harpsichords have returned to the platform. All the celebrated choral works of the 18th century and earlier such as Handel's *Messiah* and Bach's *B minor Mass* are now performed as much as possible by the instruments for which they were written. Nowadays performances of Haydn's symphonies, Handel's *Water Music*, and so on often include harpsichord continuo.

Illustrated on page 23, is the sort of figured bass upon which a harpsichordist would have to extemporize, followed by an interpretation which is impeccable in style because it comes from an impeccable source: *An Essay on the True Art of Playing Keyboard Instruments* by the son of J.S. Bach, Carl Philipp Emanuel.

Harpsichord repertoire

Some contemporary composers have made use of the intimate timbre of the harpsichord, significantly in the context of a chamber orchestra. Two examples are listed here:
Martinu: Concerto for Harpsichord and Small Orchestra
Carter: Double Concerto for Harpsichord and Piano with Two Chamber Orchestras

The
Piano

The piano is rarely used as an instrument of the orchestra, but when it is the part is written in the score between the percussion and strings. The piano is a percussion instrument since the strings are struck by hammers.

Today the piano is the heaviest of all musical instruments, the cabinet being uniformly sombre in colour and the several legs of muscular appearance on account of the weight they have to bear. Unlike any other instrument of the orchestra the name of the maker could sometimes be read by the audience because it used to be announced in large letters (see photo on page 126).

The iron framework of the concert grand carries a tension load of about 30 tons and each key needs a weight of approximately 3 oz to depress it. Translated into everyday shopping terms, a chord of five notes is equal to a one pound bag of sugar. The piano is therefore almost an athlete's instrument, a fact recognized by the celebrated pianist Dame Myra Hess who, having witnessed a particularly energetic display of pianism, barely resisted springing to her feet and calling out 'Vive le sport!'

History

Bartolomeo Cristofori (1655–1731) is popularly credited with the invention of a hammer mechanism which he built into a harpsichord-shaped cabinet, but many musicologists suggest that only the earliest extant pianos are by Cristofori, because his mechanism was too accomplished and advanced not to have trial-and-error precursors. Whether the hammer mechanism was invented in Italy or not, the fact is that after Cristofori the Italians took no further part in the development of the piano, the centres for its advance being first Germany, then France and England, and finally the U.S.

RIGHT
A drawing of the piano action. It makes possible a wide variety of effects on the part of the skillful player. When the key is only partially released, the check stops the hammer from falling all the way back, allowing rapid repetition of a note. The action of the damper can be forestalled by pedal action, allowing sostenuto, or sustained tone

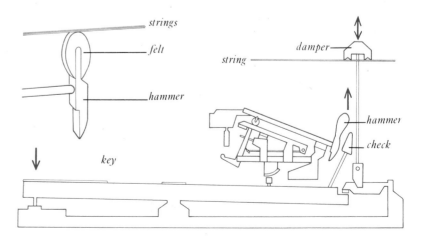

From its beginning the history of the piano is one of intense commercial rivalry, abounding in names that are familiar today: Broadwood, established in England in 1723, Erard, established in France in 1779, Chickering, established in Massachusetts in 1823, Bechstein, established in Germany in 1853, the same year as Steinway in the U.S. These are a mere five names out of more than a thousand firms producing pianos at the beginning of this century. The piano was almost as common then as the ubiquitous TV set today.

Gottfried Silberman (1683–1753) was the first successful maker (copying Cristofori's action) and his instruments were nearly all bought by Frederick the Great and housed at Sans Souci, where Quantz, J.S. Bach and C.P.E. Bach regarded and played them with

BELOW
This is what is described as an art piano. Its ebony case is inlaid with ormolu, and it is dated 1873. The firm of John Brinsmead was founded in 1836

RIGHT
A modern cross-strung upright piano with an iron frame, made by Broadwood. The firm was founded in 1723 and was one of the first famous makers of pianos, supplying Beethoven and Chopin

RIGHT
A modern cross-strung upright piano with an iron frame, made by Broadwood. The firm was founded in 1723 and was one of the first famous makers of pianos, supplying Beethoven and Chopin

FAR RIGHT
The glockenspiel

interest and enthusiasm. The piano was introduced into England just after the middle of the 18th century by yet another son of J.S. Bach, Johann Christian.

Two acute problems faced the early makers. First, what sort of sound were they trying to produce? Second, how were they to devise a reliable and fluent hammer action that would rival the action of the perfected harpsichord?

The first hammers were covered in leather, producing in some cases a reflection of harpsichord timbre. In fact some nervous early makers incorporated harpsichord and dulcimer timbres in their instruments. These faint-hearted designers were soon overtaken by those who strove to develop the small tinkle into something more robust. A plethora of patents from the 1770s onwards bears witness to the international scramble for an action that allowed of rapid repetition over a wide range of dynamics.

In the 18th century there was already one type of piano being produced in huge quantities. This was called the square piano – no one knows quite why since the cabinet is a shallow oblong box. This popular square was invented and introduced in 1760 by Johannes Zumpe, a pupil of Silberman. Square pianos were eminently suitable for accompanying the voice, having a delicate and subtle timbre. Instead of having pedals the earliest squares had hand stops, some of which damped the whole or half the strings producing a timbre not unlike that of the buff stop on the harpsichord. The lid could be half or fully closed, but there was a hinged flap at the sound board end which, when open, released the sound of the upper harmonics. All these early pianos, whether square or grand, had wooden frames. As the tension of the strings was increased to produce more volume, small areas of metal bracing were introduced at the hitch pin end to prevent warping. Fairly rapidly these areas of metal bracing were extended, and by 1820 Erard had produced the first iron bar grand piano, the iron bars running the length of the sound board. This was but a step away from the full iron frame of the type patented in 1843 by Jonas Chickering.

By the end of the 19th century there were countless shapes and sizes of piano to choose from, ranging from small folding yacht pianos

to very grand uprights with storage space for music. There were pyramid pianos and giraffe pianos (really upright grands), and pianos with up to six pedals providing different effects on the strings and bashing a drum and bells for the realistic reproduction of Turkish music. There were pianos concealed in tables and cabinets, and hosts of uprights of different sizes and specifications, not to mention the straightforward concert grands – except that they were not all that straightforward.

Whatever the shape and size of those earlier pianos, the makers always strove for elegance. The cabinets of the small squares, supported on elegantly turned legs, became collectors' pieces of furniture, and many an action was ripped out in order to convert the silent shell into something more useful such as a cocktail cabinet or dressing table. Woods were carefully chosen for their grain and craftsmen indulged in filigree fretwork for the music rack on either side of which glowed merry brass candlesticks. Some grands were decorated with brass inlay and one piano at least was made entirely of brass. Hand-pleated silk of superior quality concealed the sound board and strings of the uprights. All this contributed to making pianos desirable adornments of the home, a pleasure to look at as well as to hear. Mass production spoiled all that and all pianos began to sound alike and to look alike – hence the necessity for writing the name on the instrument as well as in the concert or recital programme.

Technique

While all other instrumentalists must know how to tune and must have a good working knowledge of the mechanics of their instruments, pianists need know none of this. The instrument is delivered or wheeled on to the platform tuned in advance and ready to play. Should a string break, a pedal fall off or the instrument get out of tune, no pianist will have with him a little bag of tools to remedy the situation, not even a tuning hammer. In any case the tension load on the strings is such that, particularly in the bass, a strong hand is needed to manipulate the tuning key and the hammering, as it is called, of a note once it is tuned in order to ensure that the wrest pin is firm, is not a job designed to improve delicate touch. The great pianists frequently have a tuner who remains in attendance throughout a recital or concert. But for the not-so-great doing perhaps their first tour, faced with anything from a clapped-out old parlour upright to a much-loved but tired grand with what is described as 'a lovely tone' (meaning generally that the felt on the hammers was packed into hard knobs years ago), the situation can be discouraging. Too late they may wish they were guitar players or flautists.

Repertoire

True piano music was not published until about 1770, the year of Beethoven's birth; even Beethoven's first sonatas were published for the harpsichord *or* pianoforte. Mozart trained on the harpsichord and did not meet a piano until 1777; by then Muzio Clementi (1752–1832) had written piano sonatas exploiting the instrument for the first time as a pianoforte, with no reference to harpsichord technique.

ABOVE
in 1932 about two dozen pianos were ordered by the BBC for the then new Broadcasting House. In this photograph craftsmen can be seen making adjustments to an action which has been withdrawn from a case, polishing, and screwing on hinges. Above on the right hang pieces of wood moulded for the bent side. The firm of Challen was established in 1804

As the mechanism of the piano improved so two schools of composition developed. The first stemmed from Clementi, who wrote exclusively for the piano. Clementi was followed by a host of other pianist-composers who developed brilliance of technique, often to the exclusion of musical thought. This could be said to have culminated in the Victorian rash of vapid *morceaux de salon*.

The other school of composition started with Clementi's rival at the keyboard, Mozart, an orchestral composer. And because orchestral composers thought in terms of varied timbres it was they who added a new dimension to the repertoire. This school to which Haydn, Beethoven and Brahms contributed, as well as Schumann and Schubert, culminated in Liszt (1811 – 1886), who in a sense bestrode both schools; he transcribed all Beethoven's symphonies, including the Ninth, for the piano.

Chopin (1810 – 1849) stands apart, the poet without peer, of whom George Sand wrote that 'he made an instrument speak the language of infinity,' adding, 'Great progress in taste and intelligence is needed before his works become popular. The day will come when his music will be orchestrated.' Sand wrote that sometime after 1847. Fortunately the prophecy of orchestration has not come true.

Just as there is no substitute for the harpsichord where harpsichord music is intended, there is no substitute for the Pleyel piano for which Chopin wrote, and the time is undoubtedly coming when there will be a restoration of performances on those more refined instruments with their delicate, water-colour sounds. But this sound provides at least one reason for the piano not being used as an instrument of the orchestra, until the 20th century: the sound had insufficient penetration.

Copeland, Shostakovich, Prokofiev and Tippett have used the modern piano in symphonies, sometimes doubling, sometimes strengthening some feature of the score. Stravinsky gave it a solo in *Petrushka* and Bartók in his *Dance Suite* used it blatantly for what it is: a percussion instrument. It is also used by Saint-Saëns in a more familiar work, *The Carnival of Animals.* Sir Michael Tippett, in his *Concerto for Orchestra* and his Third Symphony, uses the piano along with the other percussion for exotic colouring.

Piano concerti are almost outside the province of this book, unlike concerti for the violin, which is after all one of the most important instruments of the orchestra. It is hard to write anything about the piano, however, without mentioning the piano concerti of Mozart and Beethoven, both orchestral composers who were also great pianists. Beethoven's Fourth Piano Concerto, as well as one or two of Mozart's, have been recorded on original instruments. Tchaikovsky's First Piano Concerto begins with a rousing fanfare for horns, followed by one of the most famous themes in orchestral music, which is played by the orchestra while the piano merely provides a simple accompaniment. (Curiously, the tune is not heard again throughout the work.) Brahms' Second Piano Concerto is almost a sort of grand symphony in four movements with piano obbligato; it also has many good solo passages for other instruments. The amusing Second Piano Concerto of Shostakovitch uses the piano, in its first movement, as a sort of fast and furious percussion instrument.

Maurizio Pollini has made a brilliant recording of a piano reduction of pieces from Stravinsky's *Petrushka* ballet in which the brittle, percussive aspect of the modern instrument is very apparent.

Music libraries abound in vocal scores: piano reductions of celebrated opera and choral works, used mainly for the purpose of rehearsing singers. Piano reductions, of orchestral music as well, were enormously popular and profitable to publishers until the radio and the record player replaced the piano in the home.

One of Sir Michael Tippett's trademarks is the use of the piano and the harp in the orchestra to provide tonal colour and a sort of ethereal punctuation. This piano part *occurs near the beginning of the second movement of his Second Symphony; the accompanying harp part from the same passage is reproduced on page 135*

Piano repertoire

Stravinsky: *Petrushka*
Bartók: *Dance Suite*
Bartók: Sonata for Two Pianos
 and Percussion
Saint-Saëns: *Carnival of the Animals*
Tippett: *Concerto for Orchestra*
Brahms: Piano Concerto No. 2
Shostakovitch: Piano Concerto
 No. 2

THE
STRING
INSTRUMENTS

The Harp

compass of the harp

The stave for the harp is written under that of the percussion. Reading downwards it is the first stringed instrument in the score. Since it has a wide compass – of six and a half octaves – the music occupies two staves, the notation for the right hand being written in the treble clef and that of the left generally in the bass clef.

There is something lonely-looking and remote about the single harpist, by tradition usually a woman, arriving early on the platform to tune more than forty strings – some of gut or nylon, some wound wire and some copper. A blast or two of hot or cold air from an off-stage corridor can spoil her endeavours, as can the rising heat and humidity in the hall once the audience has seated itself.

The cascades of glissandi that can be played on the harp are often used to evoke the music of Heaven, suggesting a lack of creative imagination in that place, for although glissandi and arpeggio passages are characteristic of the harp, bold chords, trills, rapid repetitions on one note, harmonics and stopped notes are also part of its expressive repertoire.

The orchestral harp of today is described as a double action instrument, on account of the seven pedals at the base, each of which has two positions. When depressed one notch they raise the pitch by a semitone, and depressed another notch, by a further semitone. Since each pedal represents one note of the diatonic scale the number of combinations possible, even for one note, is considerable and in certain passages footwork can be as frantic as fingerwork. At the end of a concert the harp will be covered and, if to be transported, it will be loaded into a trunk with the strings slackened off – ready to tune all over again.

RIGHT
The association of music and food belongs to a tradition unbroken from ancient times until today, though it is debased in restaurants with piped-in music. In this Dutch painting of 1560 the small 24-string harp, probably standing on a stool, accompanies the singers and the arrival of a dish of grapes

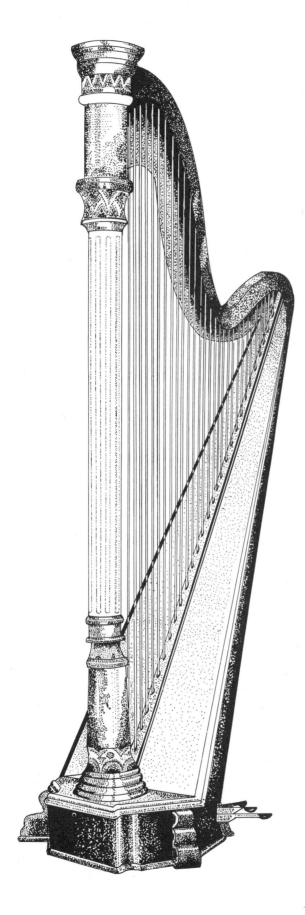

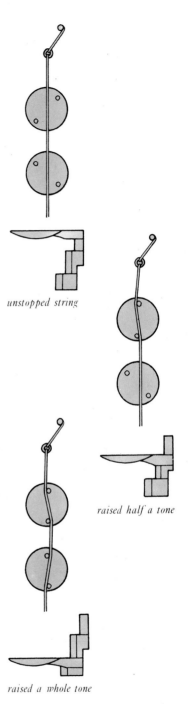

unstopped string

raised half a tone

raised a whole tone

ABOVE
*How the harp pedals work. There are
seven pedals on today's harp, one for
each diatonic note of the scale. Pedal
work has to be fast and silent, and
composers are not always terribly
considerate of the harpist! But it is
possible, for example, to play F-sharp
instead of G-flat to avoid a difficult
change*

History

The name 'harp' probably comes from the Old English word *hearp*, meaning talon, nail or plectrum. In Anglo-Saxon times the instrument was plucked. The harp is believed to have its origins in the hunting bow. The first harps had no fore-pillar and were called bow harps; these have been known for three or four thousand years.

A 7th century BC relief from Nineveh, now in the British Museum, shows a procession of Elamite harpists plucking their strings in a manner that is almost identical to that used by today's harpists. The different positions of the left hand of each harpist indicate that each musician is plucking a different note. The procession includes people clapping, a singer beating her throat (producing a sort of tremolo), and a lyre player, as well as a small drum and a pair of double reed pipes. Such a multiplicity of harps is rarely heard today, and the relief probably represents concerted music of some complexity.

There is a considerable wealth of pictorial evidence of the early existence of the harp in the Middle East, Scandinavia, Ireland and all parts of the British Isles. But there are still gaps and puzzles in the story, one of them being the date and place of the introduction of the fore-pillar, creating what is termed the 'frame harp.' This is the instrument played in the orchestra today.

Early European literature also abounds with references to the harp and to the many legends connected with it. It has been a symbol of heavenly bliss for hundreds of years. Similarly on earth it has been endowed with magical powers, its sound soothing savage breasts, driving away evil spirits and gathering audiences of bemused animals.

The tradition of singing to harp accompaniment must be as old as the instrument itself and the pleasure of it is celebrated by Chaucer in the *Canterbury Tales*. The Friar harpist 'when that he had song' is described: *His eyes twinkled in his head aright, As doon the sterres in the frosty night.*

The Anglo-Saxons strung their harps with twisted horse hair but the Irish, who experimented with the shape of the instrument and were acclaimed throughout Europe for their harping, used gold, silver and brass. The Irish played low-headed harps, with large sound-boards sometimes carved from one block of willow, which were played with the finger nails and produced a strong, clear, bell-like sound. This was the type of harp that could be hung in trees at times of grief: hung where a breeze can blow across the strings, a strange and ghostly music is produced.

An immense variety of harps have been played in different countries at different times. One of the most important is the triple harp, a high-headed frame type with three ranks of strings, the outer two providing the diatonic notes of the scale and the inner, the accidentals. This was known in the 14th century and was the first fully chromatic harp. Like the old Irish harp it had a clear, bell-like sound, the technique in this case being to strike rather than to pluck or pull the strings. It was played well into the 20th century in Wales and was known as the Welsh harp. The only known scoring for it was in Handel's *Esther* (1720).

It is generally believed that the first pedal harp was invented by the

LEFT
*An imaginative Victorian engraving
of a fresco, showing an Egyptian
harpist, painted in the sepulchres
of Thebes*

Bavarian Simon Hochbrucker between 1720 and 1740. It had a single-action hook mechanism connected to the pedals by wires and was thoroughly unreliable since it pulled the strings out of alignment and broke them. This harp was popular until Sebastian Erard (1752 – 1831) replaced the hooks with a pronged disk which did not interfere with the alignment.

The first pedal harps adorned all aristocratic and fashionable homes, and the great luthiers or instrument makers were engaged in their manufacture – Lepine, Naderman and Cousineau among them. Many of these magnificent instruments are now only to be seen in museums, behind glass, untouchable and silent since they have become too frail to play. It was Cousineau who was the first to introduce a form of double action, but Sebastian Erard again improved upon it and altered the harp's configuration to give it greater strength. Erard's system, used world-wide today, consists of pedals connected to rods which pass up the fore-pillar and work pronged disks.

RIGHT
A close-up of the hands of a harpist

Technique

The strings of the harp are pulled or plucked with the tips of the fingers; all fingers except the little ones are used. The strings are plucked in the middle to produce the normal sound and near the sound-board for a somewhat metallic timbre.

Harmonics are produced by stopping the string half way up and plucking the upper portion; normally only the first harmonic, the octave, is called for. Rather dry sounds can be produced by stopping the strings with the hand immediately after plucking them; these are called *sons etouffés*. Raising and lowering the pitch of the strings by means of the double action of pedal and disk mechanism calls for rapid yet inaudible footwork.

All harpists carry with them a second set of strings or at least a selection of the major ones. These are colour-coded to assist identification. Strings are inclined to break – noisily in a bar of silence if Fate is unkind – and harpists must be able to re-string rapidly and retune.

Repertoire

Garner Read, who collated the *Thesaurus of Orchestral Devices*, wrote of the harp: 'It is safe to say that no other orchestral instrument is so generally misunderstood by orchestrators and composers and so ill-used in the overwhelming majority of modern works . . . To the average orchestrator the harp unfortunately means but one thing – glissando, and more glissando!' Liszt was in fact the first composer to write glissandi for the harp, in his *Mephisto Waltz*. Berlioz of course had no less than ten harps in the *Damnation of Faust*, and Wagner contributed to the opulence of *Der Ring des Nibelungen* by scoring for six harps in all four operas in the cycle. But normally only one or two harps are seen in the orchestra. Perhaps it is some race

memory of the ancient Celtic and Scandinavian harps that have made French and Finnish composers the most sensitive to the expressive powers of the harp. *The Swan of Tuonela* must be one of the most celebrated of all harp pieces, but in his First Symphony Sibelius also wrote a challenging part for the harp, requiring a lot of pedal changes. Debussy scored for two harps in the *Prélude à l'Après-midi d'un Faune* using, apart from the ubiquitous glissando, chords, spread chords and harmonics.

Both Debussy and Ravel were commissioned by harp makers to write for the instrument and in 1906 Ravel published his *Introduction and Allegro* for flute, clarinet, harp and strings, a work which the American harpist Roslyn Rensch has described as 'a master lesson in harp composition.'

One of the most popular and familiar of all harp passages is a cadenza in the 'Waltz of the Flowers' from Tchaikovsky's *Nutcracker*.

The variety of sounds and effects possible on the harp and achieved in solo harp music in, for instance, Berio's *Sequenza* for solo harp, has rarely been exploited in orchestral music.

This passage for solo harp, all in the treble clef, is from the same part of   *Tippett's Second Symphony as the piano part on page 127*

Harp repertoire
Liszt: *Mephisto Waltz*
Berlioz: *Damnation of Faust*
Wagner: *Der Ring des Nibelungen*
Sibelius: *The Swan of Tuonela*
Sibelius: Symphony No. 1
Debussy: *Prélude à l'Après-midi d'un Faune*
Debussy: *Danse Sacrée et Danse Profane*
Ravel: *Introduction and Allegro*
Tchaikovsky: 'Waltz of the Flowers' from the *Nutcracker*
Berio: *Sequenza*

The Violin

compass of the violin

The part for the first violins, the first and the most important of the bowed string instruments, is written in the score in the treble clef on a stave above the second violins. The strings of the violin are tuned to G D A E and have a compass of $3\frac{1}{2}$ octaves. Until fairly recently some orchestras preferred to have their violins strung exclusively with gut, but the thin top string has a tendency to break easily, so it has been replaced by wire, tuned by a small sensitive screw on the tail piece. Today a violin might be strung entirely with metal, each string having a tail piece screw, or some strings may be gut wound with aluminium, silver or copper.

The variety of sounds and effects that can be produced from the violin exceeds that of any other single instrument of the orchestra, but owing to what is called a *formant* it is always possible to identify the violin as being the source.

Each instrument in the orchestra has its own formant. This is a particular range of harmonics which is always present to a greater or lesser degree whatever fundamental or note is played. The formant of the violin is in the three to six thousand frequency range. It is really a sort of basic body vibration code and determines the timbre of the instrument throughout its compass. Every human voice also has a formant, which enables us to identify friends or foes whether they are heard talking on the telephone, muttering the shopping list, or broadcasting. A badly made violin with a feeble formant which is not well-distributed about the body will sound poorly. A good violin with a well-balanced formant, evenly distributed over the whole complex body – which consists of over 70 separate pieces – will have a rich and satisfying timbre.

When a violin string is bowed or plucked, the vibrations are conveyed by way of the bridge to the belly and ribs of the instrument and, by means of the soundpost within the violin, to the back. On

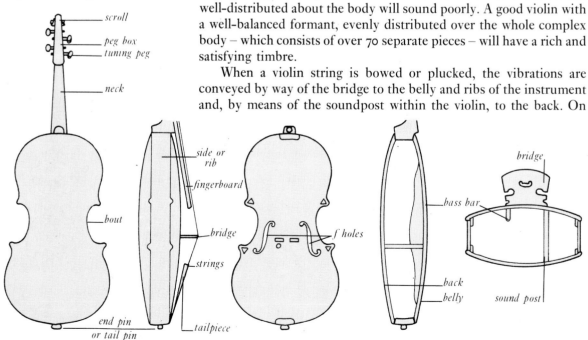

either side of the bridge are *f* holes which help to release and project the sound. One reason why some conductors do not like to place the second violins on their right is that the players are then tilting the *f* holes toward the back of the orchestra instead of to the audience.

History

'Catguts, Scrapers, Men of Rosin, Squeakers' or 'scurvy thrashing scraping Mongrels.' That is how the itinerant fiddlers of the 17th century were described, and this serves as a shocking reminder that those sober-suited violinists massed importantly in the front line of the symphony orchestra have neither a particularly old nor an entirely respectable history.

The history of the bowed string instruments is another of those tangles of stray possibilities which do not unravel into a logical story. From the 11th century onwards musicologists are confronted by a variety of bowed chordophones in sculptures and pictures and a confusion of names in literature and music. Evidence however

ABOVE
Silhouettes showing the relative size difference between the violin and the viola

suggests that the origin of bowed instruments lies not in those that were plucked but in those that were struck. It is, after all, a logical step from striking a string with a stick to scraping it.

The first known use of the word 'vyollon' has been traced back to 1520, but the modern spelling was not used until 1537. This name derives from *fides* – string. In northern languages this led to vielle, fithele, fithel and fiddle; in the south, to fidula, vidula, vihuela, viol and through vyollon to violin. In the middle of the 17th century, when the design of the violin had been evolved by the makers of Cremona, a distinction was made between 'melodious rogues' who played the fiddle for feasts, dancing and other forms of lawful and unlawful entertainment, and violinists who played serious or composed music.

By the time of Monteverdi (1567–1643) the Amati family of Cremona was established and was to dominate violin making for the next hundred years. Nicola Amati died in 1684 and he was succeeded by

his disciple Antonio Stradivari (c. 1640–1737). By the time Stradivari died the perfected violin had emerged as an important solo instrument as well as an instrument of the orchestra. Viols and viol music now faded away, although signs of their dominion lingered on a while. In the Brandenburg Concerti, written between 1717 and 1723, J.S. Bach scored for viola da braccia (violin supported by the arm) and viola da gamba (larger and supported by the leg or ankle). The original compass of the consort of viols was founded on the compasses of the different human voices – soprano, alto, tenor, and bass – and that division of bowed string instruments became and has remained the foundation of the symphony orchestra.

In the seething cauldron of social and political events of the late 18th century, music and musical instruments were themselves revolutionized. Pitch, tuning, volume and technique were all coming under close scrutiny. The orchestra itself was growing in size, and playing to larger audiences, and the art of orchestration was developing. The violin, like the viol in its time, was now considered too small-voiced. From about 1770 therefore the violins of the Cremonese school and those made later to the same dimensions were modified to produce greater volume and brilliance. The sound post was made stouter, the bass bar enlarged and the neck lengthened and thrown back a few degrees. The bridge was also made more arched to take the higher tension of the strings, this having risen from 63 lb to 90 lb. Simultaneously the bow was re-designed.

The earliest bow resembled a hunting bow, with a pronounced convex stick. In the 1600s the curve was modified and the tip partially straightened. In Corelli's time (1653–1713) the bow was a good deal shorter than it is today, and somewhat more rigid. Tartini (1692–1770) lengthened the stick and made it thinner and therefore more elastic. But it was François Tourte (1747–1835) who evolved the bow that is used today – longer, lighter, more flexible and with a concave stick. This bow introduced greater control over a wider dynamic range and had altogether much more bounce and life about it. The ribbon has always been made of horse hair; according to one expert, the hair from the tail of the stallion is best of all since it is less greasy than that of the mare. Experiments with substitute materials have failed. The chin rest also introduced some time in the 18th century, reportedly by the violinist and composer Louis Spohr (1784–1859).

Violinists will often refer to the *purfling* on their instruments. This is a bordering of the profile of the belly or back or both, with inlay. Its purpose is to give more elasticity to the body of the instrument. The mute, on the other hand, which has been known since Lully's time, does just the opposite. The mute is a small metal comb that is clamped on to the top of the bridge. The weight impedes a number of vibrations from reaching the body of the violin and thus an attenuated sound is produced.

Today violinists in the orchestra all play the type of instrument evolved during the 18th century, with a Tourte design bow. The more fortunate among them possess original but modified violins of the Cremonese school. These fetch very high prices in the auction rooms today. In the last century £200 to £500 (then about $800 to $2000) was

considered to be an excessive price for a Guarnerius or an Amati for, it was pointed out, the principal violin makers of the late 19th century, Thibouville-Lamy, with extensive premises in London and Paris, manufactured and sold violins for four shillings and sixpence (then about one dollar) *and* made a profit of 15%.

FAR LEFT
A modern orchestral pedal harp

ABOVE
The violins of the London Symphony Orchestra

Technique

Rank and file violinists need to possess a technique that is almost equal to that of a soloist. Back desk players are no less important than those at the front of the double file, and playing second fiddle is not necessarily the lowly and subservient role implied by the common expression. All orchestral violinists have to have a wide repertoire of fingering and bowing techniques, many of which they will have to demonstrate if they are called to audition for a place in an orchestra.

The violinist makes his own notes and from the start is taught seven basic positions for the left hand fingering of the strings; these positions correspond to the seven diatonic notes of the scale. Each position provides sixteen diatonic notes – four to a string. An advanced student will learn half positions. Crisp and fast chromatic scales, such as can be played on the piano, are not possible on the violin. The experienced and celebrated violinist Carl Flesch (1873–1944) was able to write a large book devoted exclusively to the subject of fingering alone; it is clearly not a subject whose intricacies can be tackled in this book.

Like fingering, bowing is an art of some complexity which has developed gradually over the centuries. Only the more obvious orchestral devices can be described here.

There is a difference in sound between an up and a down bow because of the way the bow is held, it being possible to exert more pressure at the heel than at the tip. For emphasis a down bow is used, and for passages consisting of a series of powerful strokes, the part of the bow near the heel is used. The up bow is less emphatic and the tip is used for light, quiet passages. Long full bows are used for *legato*, and short bows for *spiccato* or *saltando*, both forms of bouncing bow. A common device is *tremolo*, more graphically and simply described as scrubbing. Composers sometimes indicate the type of bowing they want, but on the whole they leave it to the discretion of the violinists and/or the conductor.

Double-stopping consists of playing two strings in harmony, each string being fingered differently. Unisons (the same note on two strings) are also produced in this manner. On account of the arching of the bridge it is not possible to play on more than two strings at a time and chords consisting of three or four notes have to be spread. Chords of harmonics are not possible. Harmonics are produced by lightly touching the string and lightly bowing.

The plucked sound of the strings was originally a substitute for mandoline sounds, and therefore *pizzicato* is the least original of violin playing devices, although there are original devices such as pizzicato with the left hand, with the strings bowed at the same time. *Tremolando*, or strumming, is also typical of plucked string instruments like the guitar.

The sound of harmonics has an ethereal quality, but bowing very close to the bridge – *sul ponticello* – or over the fingerboard – *sul tasto* – produce other degrees of attenuated timbres. A more unusual and rather skinny sound is produced by bowing, striking or plucking the portion of string between the bridge and the tail piece. *Col legno* means 'with the wood', and a desiccated sound is produced by striking the sounding length of the string with the stick of the bow.

Some of the terms used for violin strokes are reminders of the fact the fiddle was used to teach dancing – *jeté*, *louré*, *sautillé* – but on the whole the terms used today are Italian in origin, some of them being borrowed from singing – *cantabile*, *mezza* and *sotto voce* and *portamento*.

The use of the mute is indicated by the words *con sordine* in most scores, but in English the word mute is used and this should not be confused with the Italian *muta*, which means change, and is used to indicate to a player that he is to change instruments, from flute to piccolo for example, or from oboe to cor anglais.

The *accordatura* of the violin is the ordinary tuning, but *scordatura* indicates a different tuning; this device is found more in 20th century than 19th century works and it is used to enable the violinist to perform more unusual passage work or, on occasion, to produce a different timbre. But the music of Heinrich Ignaz Franz von Biber (1644–1704), himself an expert string player, abounds in alternative tuning, making possible a great variety of unusual double-stops.

ABOVE
An old-fashioned drawing supposed to illustrate the violinist's stance. In fact a violin teacher would probably tell him that his left wrist should be held flat, and in any case he appears to be sawing away on the bridge!

Mozart's *Sinfonia Concertante* for violin and viola also contains scordatura.

Repertoire

The orchestral repertoire for the violin is vast and varied in every respect. There is such a host of well-loved violin concerti performed by popular soloists all over the world that it is unnecessary to list them. In addition there are countless orchestral compositions which feature the solo violin, such as Rimsky-Korsakov's *Schéhérazade*, in which the violin portrays the storyteller herself, or the second movement of Mahler's Fourth Symphony, in which the solo instrument is tuned a semitone high, so as to give it a slightly demonic flavour. And there are also many works specifically worth mentioning because they introduce the listener to some of the special effects in the violinist's bag of tricks.

Mozart's 'Jupiter' Symphony and Rossini's overture to *La Scale di Seta* include types of bowing called *marcato* or *martelé* ('hammered'). (In Rossini's overture to *Il Signor Bruschino*, the players are instructed to tap on their desks with their bows.) There are good passages of staccato in Beethoven's First and Fifth Symphonies. Saltando, or bouncing bow, occurs in Rimsky-Korsakov's *Schéhérazade*. Two unusual forms of pizzicato, as well as passages sul ponticello, occur in Bartók's *Music for Strings, Percussion and Celesta*: in the first the pizzicato is produced with the fingernail, and in the second the string is pulled hard enough to cause it to rebound off the finger board. Col legno occurs in both Copland's Four Dance Episodes from *Rodeo* and in Mahler's First Symphony. The use of sul tasto, like many of these curiously weedy or rather thin sounds, belongs to the later composers such as Ravel, in his version of *Schéhérazade*, and Mahler in *Das Lied von der Erde*. Schoenberg's *Pierrot Lunaire*, a revolutionary work also mentioned in the section on Voice, requires a number of special effects, including sul ponticello, natural harmonics and the use of specific strings for certain passages.

Two major and more familiar works exclusively for strings, Elgar's *Introduction and Allegro* and Bartók's *Divertimento for String Orchestra*, give by contrast an idea of the different ways of writing for strings: the first being based on the classical tradition and the second on the more rugged and adventurous traditional techniques, in this case those of the Balkans. These peasants with their horny hands, stiff it would seem from manual labour, have an important place in the history of violin technique. Those who have heard them, such as Liszt, Bartók and Kodály, have been inspired by their vivacity and their varied forms of bowing and chording, often only made possible by the fact that some of them never abandoned the flatter bridge.

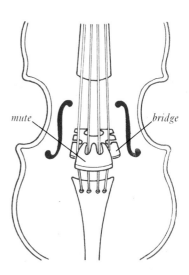

ABOVE
A violin with the mute in place on the bridge. The mute can be made of wood, bone, metal or other materials; it absorbs some of the vibrations before they are transmitted to the body of the instrument. Its purpose is not just to make the violins play quietly: the orchestral violinist is capable of doing that without a mute. The device changes the tonal quality of the sound; a forte on muted strings may be just what the composer wants

This solo violin part is from Rimsky-Korsakov's Schéhérazade; it   *is the seductive voice of the storyteller herself*

Violin repertoire

Rimsky–Korsakov:
  Schéhérazade
Mahler: Symphony No. 4
Rossini: Overture, *La Scala di Seta*
Rossini: Overture, *Il Signor Bruschino*
Bartók: *Music for Strings, Percussion and Celesta*
Bartók: *Divertimento for String Orchestra*
Elgar: *Introduction and Allegro*
Tippett: *Concerto for Double String Orchestra*
Ravel: *Schéhérazade*
Copland: Four Dance Episodes from *Rodeo*
Enesco: *Roumanian Rhapsodies*
Concerti by Bach, Beethoven, Mendelssohn, Brahms, Tchaikovsky, Sibelius, Bartók, Berg, Shostakovich, Shoenberg

The *Viola*

compass of the viola

Viola players sit in a group left or right centre of the conductor. Their strings are tuned to C G D A. The upper two are plain gut, the others wound wire; some players prefer all wound strings.

The viola has a somewhat melancholy timbre which has been little exploited in either solo or orchestral music. By early tradition the viola was 'of little importance in the musical establishment' (Quantz, 1752) and viola players were 'always taken from among the refuse of violinists' (Berlioz). Fingering for the viola is the same as for the violin but because the instrument is larger it requires a stronger hand with a bigger stretch. The bow is also larger and heavier than that of the violin.

History

There have always been different sizes and types of viola, as well as different names – violino, violetta, cinquième, quinte de violon and so on. But the orchestral viola is an abbreviation of viola da braccio (arm viola) and it is still called *Bratsche* in German. At the time of the great Cremonese makers of stringed instruments, Amati and Guarneri were making violas with a body length of $16\frac{1}{4}$ inches. Later violas were made between 17 to $18\frac{1}{2}$ inches long, but by Mozart's time a mere 14 to 15 inches. The Lionel Tertis version, first made in 1930, is $16\frac{3}{4}$ inches long. In the opinion of many makers and musicians the problem of the relationship between size and volume of sound of the viola has not yet been satisfactorily resolved. This can be seen to be true because in no one orchestra are all the violas of the same dimensions.

The story of the viola is a sad one from which historians can wring little excitement. Interest in it in the first half of the 18th century was so feeble that there were hardly any violas made at all and it was not until string quartets became popular that the better performers began to brush up their technique.

Champions of the viola have admittedly emerged from time to time, the Bohemian Karl Stamitz (1746–1801) in particular. The Stamitz family were celebrated in the 18th century; in fact, the town of Mannheim, where they lived, was a strong contender with Vienna for importance in the development of classical music. Karl, who was a viola player, rescued the instrument from its obscurity by writing independent parts for it in his symphonies and by writing a viola concerto. Haydn, Mozart, Beethoven and Schubert had all played the viola and recognized its potential, but mainly for chamber music for which they were more or less assured of skilled performers. In symphonic works, wrote Berlioz, 'it was unfortunately impossible . . . to write anything for violas of a prominent character, requiring even ordinary skill in execution.' It was due to Berlioz that, after some years of wrangling, a viola class was established at the Paris Conservatoire.

That was not until 1894, when half the world's great symphonic music had already been written, and Lionel Tertis, the outstanding protagonist of the viola, was already eighteen years old.

More than anyone else it was Tertis, a great player and a fine musician, who brought the viola respectability. He badgered composers to write for him, and himself transcribed violin and cello concerti for the viola. In an attempt to overcome the weakness of the volume-to-size ratio of the instrument, Tertis redesigned the viola, but without ultimate success. Tertis was succeeded by other players, such as Bernard Shore, who also achieved international reputations. The viola section of the orchestra is today equal to any other string section in technical ability, and this is demonstrated by the quality and difficulty of the music now written for it.

BELOW
Lionel Tertis playing the viola he designed

Repertoire

Paganini played the viola, and it was for him that Berlioz wrote the extended solo in *Harold in Italy* – although Paganini never actually performed it. By the time of Elgar's *Enigma Variations* (1899), the sound of the viola peeps out quite boldly in the sixth and twelfth variations. The third movement of Kodály's *Háry János Suite* begins with an extended viola solo. Bartók, whose string writing is never less than interesting and sometimes outrageous, wrote a viola concerto (1945). So did Walton (1929, revised 1961) and Copland (1957). Hindemith, a distinguished viola soloist as well as a composer and teacher, wrote for viola and orchestra including a concerto (1935). Walton dedicated his concerto to Hindemith. For good measure, the first movement and the finale of Copland's First Symphony both begin with viola solos.

FAR LEFT
The violas of the Chicago Symphony Orchestra conducted by Sir George Solti

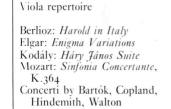

In this passage from the third movement of Beethoven's Fifth Symphony, the viola section,   *accompanied by the bassoons, joins the basses and the cellos in the powerful theme reproduced on page 161*

Viola repertoire

Berlioz: *Harold in Italy*
Elgar: *Enigma Variations*
Kodály: *Háry János Suite*
Mozart: *Sinfonia Concertante*, K.364
Concerti by Bartók, Copland, Hindemith, Walton

The Cello

compass of the cello

There are fewer cellos in the orchestra than violins because a cello produces a larger volume of sound than a violin. Cellists sit either to the right of the conductor or, if the second violins are placed there, in front of him.

The cello being derived from the viola da gamba, which was supported by the leg, it appears to be clutched and supported by the knees; in fact the weight is taken to the floor by a spike. The compass of the cello is five octaves, and the strings are tuned an octave lower than those of the viola: C G D A. The first two strings are of gut and the others wound, although there is today a tendency to use metal for all four strings.

All members of the violin family are acoustic resonators or boxes over which strings are stretched; the resonators amplify the sound of the agitated strings. The size, shape and material of the resonator determines the timbre that the strings will produce. Any box that is strung will respond in some measure (fiddles have been made from cigar boxes and sardine tins). But if the box is given curves, vaulting, a sound post to conduct the sound and *f* holes to allow them to escape, the box becomes a musical instrument. The eventual shape of all the instruments of the violin family is no less than a miracle of acoustic design which was already arrived at in the 16th century. One of the

RIGHT
The body of a cello under construction, with the front of the instrument removed. The sound post is not shown

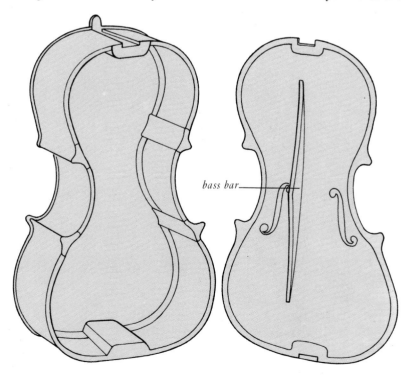

bass bar

earliest known cellos is dated 1572 and it is by Andrea Amati of Cremona.

Every fraction of an inch of the cello is calculated to contribute to fine, resonant tone. The body is about an inch short of four feet high and the sounding string length a bit over 27 inches. The *bouts* are not really knee holes but part of the acoustic design. Various woods are used, and different woods for different parts – pear, sycamore and maple being the favourites. Since all trees make a different density of wood according to the season, one of the purposes of the varnish is to assist towards an even distribution of the vibrations that course through the varying densities. Too heavy a varnish would make the wood rigid; too light a varnish

would fail to be effective. All the woods are weathered naturally, being stacked in the open air today much in the same way as they have been for centuries. Oven-fresh wood, dried in a kiln, is useless. And it is worth mentioning that it can take up to ten years to 'play in' any instrument of the violin family. If a cello is laid aside for any length of time it will need playing in again. Even after a day of silence it needs limbering up; part of the purpose of all that playing that goes on before the concert starts is to bring the whole instrument alive. Musical instruments enjoy being played.

History

The name violoncello is a diminutive of violone, a larger instrument of somewhat uncertain history and purpose.

The cello did not gain instant success either as a solo instrument or as a member of the orchestra. There was a long tussle for supremacy between gamba and cello fanciers. The French thought the cello too noisy and in 1740 Hubert de Blanc published a book with the expansive title *Défense de la Basse de Viole contre les entreprises du*

ABOVE
Frederick, Prince of Wales, plays a viola da gamba, or leg viol, supported by the knees. His sisters accompany him on harpsichord and mandolin. The picture, painted in 1733 by Philip Mercier, is called A Music Party

LEFT
In this close-up of a cellist the thumb is being used for fingering. As always with string instruments, the hair of the bow is not drawn flat across the strings

violon et les prétensions du violoncelle, in which he expressed his deep disapproval of 'the thick strings demanding exaggerated pressure of the bow, and a tension that makes them shrill.' But according to Roger North writing in 1728, the cello had been 'a very hard and harsh sounding Base, and nothing so soft and sweet as now.'

Music expressly for the cello was not written until the latter part of the 17th century, and then only to double the bass line. Beethoven was the first to exploit it as an individual voice of the orchestra.

Technique

Each string of each instrument of the violin family has its own characteristic timbre. With the cello, if there is too much crossing over from string to string in the course of a passage it can sound choppy. Since the cello is supported by a spike and not by the left hand, fingering can include the thumb; thus more notes can be produced from one position on one string. So although bowing, the 'soul' of playing, is the same as for the violin and viola, fingering is not.

Apart from each string having a different timbre, open strings sound different from stopped ones. The former have a somewhat inanimate sound partly because no vibrato can be produced from them, although a feeble reflection of this can be produced by doing vibrato on an adjacent string. Composers sometimes specify which string they want played, or if they want the particular sound of an open string.

Harmonics, which Rimsky-Korsakov considered ornamental but not essential, are impressive from a cello on account of the thickness of the strings and size of the body of the instrument. But if the spike of the cello were stuck in cotton wool there would be less resonance; the staging of a concert platform is often an acoustic resonator in itself and responds to a whole band of frequencies. Drums, the double bass and the cello are the only instruments of the orchestra that gain additional resonance from the floor.

All string players carry 'the residuary gum of turpentine (itself an oleoresin from coniferous trees) after distillation' – in other words a block of opaque brown rosin. This is rubbed along the bow hair giving it a sticky grip that helps to set the strings vibrating. The to and fro of the bow produces a fine dust of sticky rosin particles on the strings and belly of the instrument, particularly about the bridge; and string players will wipe it away at the end of a performance.

Repertoire

The voice of the cello blends and contrasts exceptionally well with all instruments while still maintaining an authority all its own; it was much used in early music as a continuo instrument. There is a strength in the attack of the bowed notes, a fullness in the pizzicato and a sweetness in the sonority of the full compass, even in the highest register; the cello contributes perhaps more than any other single instrument to the richness of the timbre of the full orchestra.

The repertoire includes some of the most tuneful and powerfully emotional concerti ever written for strings. Those by Dvořák and Elgar are probably the most familiar, while those by Haydn, Schumann and Saint-Saëns are also popular. It is remarkable how many piano concerti contain important and exposed passages for the cello. Beethoven's Fourth and Fifth, the Andante of Brahms' Second, Rachmaninoff's Second and Third provide examples, as do piano concerti by Grieg, Liszt and Piston, among others. The symphonies of Mahler are cello-spotters' delights, as is his *Das Lied von der Erde*. The symphonies of Sibelius too are frequently coloured by outstanding passages for solo cello, as is his violin concerto.

As for the violin, the full range of bowing and other effects are written for the cello by the later composers such as Bartók, Kodály and Stravinsky, whose *Firebird* suite includes sul ponticello, col legno, harmonics, pizzicato and sul tasto, among other techniques.

Any selection from this vast repertoire is bound to be subjective, and not everyone agrees on the merits of Elgar's *Enigma Variations* (so-called because the theme was never revealed by Elgar and no one has yet indentified it, although a number of theories have been advanced) but they do contain the unmistakable voice of the solo cello.

This lovely cello melody is from the slow movement of Brahms' Second Piano Concerto

Cello repertoire

Brahms: Concerto for Violin and Cello ('Double' concerto)
Brahms: Piano Concerto No. 2
Sibelius: Violin Concerto
Weber: Aria, *Und ob die Wolke sie verhülle* from *Der Freischütz*
Stravinsky: *Firebird* suite
Elgar: *Enigma Variations*
Cello concerti by Dvořák, Elgar, Schumann, Saint–Saëns and Haydn

The Double Bass

compass of the double bass

The part for the double bass is written on the bottom stave of the score. The notes sound an octave lower than written. Unlike any other member of the violin family the strings are tuned in fourths – GDAE; this is because with strings of such length and thickness the intervals between the stopped notes are very wide and if they were tuned to the usual fifths there would be insuperable physical difficulties in fingering. The greater length of thicker string gives a smaller, not wider, compass on account of the notes being so widely spaced. The compass is about two and a quarter octaves.

Bassists may appear to stand behind their tall instruments but in fact they are usually perched on high stools, frequently on an elevated section of the staging, to the right of the conductor. The weight of the instrument is taken by an adjustable peg to the floor. It is noticeable that whether there are two, ten or twenty bassists, no one instrument will have precisely the same configuration as its neighbour. All have sloping shoulders and flat backs, features retained from the viol which are purely functional; high, broad shoulders would make it impossible to reach over to finger and bow the strings. The tuning pegs are also different from those of other members of the family because instead of sticking out on either side of the scroll, they jut out at the back. And the tension of the strings is such that a cogwheel mechanism is used for adjusting the tuning.

Not only does the double bass resemble the viol in appearance, but until comparatively recently actual bowing techniques were similar, the hand being held palm facing outwards. And the stick of the bow remained convex long after other members of the family had adopted the concave Tourte type. Two ways of holding the bow are still in practice: the German, in which the bow is held like a wood saw, and the French, in which it is held like the cello bow.

History

It has been suggested that the double bass is so-called because its original role in church and instrumental music was to double the bass line. The instrument dates from the first half of the 16th century. During its career it has been made in many different sizes and the number of strings has varied from three to six. At first it was played exclusively in church where it doubled the 16 foot pipe of the organ, to marvellous effect, it is said. Then in the 17th century it was introduced to theatre orchestras. By the 18th century the Paris Opéra could boast of one which, according to one source, played only on Fridays, the day of the most important social gathering of the week.

It was a performer rather than a composer who liberated the bass from its doubling, the charming and eccentric virtuoso Domenico Dragonetti (1755–1846) who, on his death bed, 'held out his great

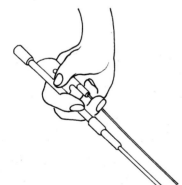

ABOVE
An early method of holding the bow, in which the third finger touches the hair and produces a singing vibrato

hand covered with callosities and unnaturally spread from constant playing and said with emotion 'This is the hand which Beethoven our great friend . . . bade me press' (Grove). Not only was Dragonetti a friend of Beethoven, but of Haydn also, and such was the span of his life that he was also heard and admired by Berlioz. During his lifetime therefore Dragonetti was involved in playing most of the new, exposed and important orchestral passages that were written for the liberated instrument. Dragonetti's instrument, like those of other virtuosi, was smaller and more manageable than that of modern orchestral players.

The composer and conductor Bottesini (1821–89) was known as the greatest player of all time and the conductor Koussevitsky (1876–1951) was also a brilliant performer. In our day the composer

ABOVE
This rather formal portrait was supposed to illustrate music making in the home. The bow is of the hand-saw type

G. Drucker plays a five-string double bass in the Philharmonia Orchestra

ABOVE LEFT
This photograph shows clearly the cog-wheel tuning mechanism of the double bass

RIGHT
The viola and the violin, with their bows

Oliver Knussen first made his name as a bassist. Today's best-known protagonist of the double bass as a solo instrument is Gary Karr, who plays an instrument which once belonged to Koussevitsky.

Two names from popular music might also be mentioned: Jimmy Blanton, who played with Duke Ellington until his early death from tuberculosis, revolutionized the playing of the instrument with his technique and delicacy he could make the whole band sound as though it were walking on tip-toe. And Charlie Mingus, who died in 1979, was second to none in his mastery of his instrument.

Technique

Unnaturally spread hands covered with 'callosities' seem likely to be the reward for a life-time of playing an instrument as heavily strung as the bass. It is a tiring instrument to play and scores will generally be found to contain bursts of energetic activity interspersed with rests or less tiring passages. Sometimes long, rapid passages are shared between firsts and seconds for ease of execution, and to prevent bassists having to fudge their way through passages they find too difficult.

As with the other bowed string instruments two types of harmonics can be produced. These are *natural* harmonics produced

when the open string is lightly touched, and *artificial* when produced from a stopped string. The former sound well from the bass but the latter do not and are rarely if ever used. The mute is also rarely used as it stifles the timbre in a way that composers find not particularly useful. Pizzicato on the other hand has a noble and resonant sound and is much used. All the bowings used on the other stringed instruments are possible but cannot be executed with as much agility because some effort is needed to overcome the inertia of a heavy string; it is slow to 'speak.'

Repertoire

When Dragonetti was trying out a bass by Gasparo de Salo (1540–1609), the greatest of all bass makers and a contemporary of Amati (c. 1511–1579), he was staying in a monastery. On the midnight the poor monks were awakened by the sound of a terrible storm – imitated on the bass by Dragonetti. This incident is a reminder of the celebrated passage in the fourth movement of Beethoven's 'Pastoral' Symphony in which the bass imitates the rumblings of the approaching storm.

In Haydn's *Creation* the bass becomes a whale, and in Saint-Saëns 'Carnival of the Animals' it takes the part of an elephant. But its more serious contributions in works by Mahler, Stravinsky and Strauss demand considerable agility. Double bass solos are very rare, but can be heard in Rimsky-Korsakov's *Schéhérazade*, Mahler's Fourth Symphony and Copland's Four Dance Episodes from the ballet *Rodeo*, as well as in Ravel's *L'Enfant et les Sortilèges*, where it is heard unaccompanied. Among the most familiar and impressive passages for double bass is that in the Scherzo of Beethoven's Fifth Symphony, where the basses burst forth with a vigorous theme. Brahms' First Symphony is also rich in writing for the bass, especially the famous pizzicatto passages in the last movement.

Double bass repertoire

Beethoven: Symphony No. 5
Beethoven: Symphony No. 6
Haydn: *Creation*
Saint–Saëns: *Carnival of the Animals*
Rimsky-Korsakov: *Schéhérazade*
Mahler: Symphony No. 4
Copland: Four Dance Episodes from *Rodeo*
Ravel: *L'Enfant et les Sortilèges*

LEFT
This vigorous theme, considered nearly unplayable when it was new, is played by the basses and cellos in the third movement of Beethoven's Fifth Symphony, joined in the seventh bar by the violas and bassoons (see page 149)

The Voice

soprano and treble (boy's voice)

mezzo–soprano

alto (and counter-tenor)

tenor (sounding an octave lower than written)

baritone

bass

Almost without exception the earlier forms of instruments described in this book were considered ideal when their timbre most closely resembled that of the human voice. A singing quality was always sought, even from the first pianos as well as from trombones, bassoons and bowed string instruments. And different members of families of instruments are still named as though they were singers – soprano, alto, tenor, baritone and bass. The compasses of the various human voices have in fact provided the foundation for the disposition of the instrumental voices in the orchestra.

As the orchestra and orchestration evolved, the concept of the human singing voice as the ideal sound began to be replaced by one based on the exhilarating contrasts and blending of different timbres. Thus each instrument became developed for its own particular characteristic quality of sound. Then the compasses of each instrument were gradually extended upwards and downwards, breaking away from the old tradition that limited them to a range comparable to that of the human voice. This was a process of liberation that took something like a hundred years. By 1891 Rimsky-Korsakov wrote triumphantly: 'Our age is one of brilliance and picturesqueness in orchestral colour. Berlioz, Glinka, Liszt, Wagner...Delibes, Bizet... Borodin, Balakirev, Glazounov and Tchaikovsky – have guided this aspect of art to the zenith of its brilliance; from this point of view they have overshadowed the preceding colourists: Weber, Meyerbeer and Mendelssohn, to whose genius they yet remain indebted for their own progress.'

It was time to re-introduce the human voice into the orchestra, but now as an additional colour rather than as the bearer of a text, by wordless singing or vocalise.

Vocalise is among the most ancient forms of singing. In religious music it is known to go back to the third century AD. It is a manner of singing in which a vowel or a syllable is drawn out or extended by ornamentation. Some religious groups believed that this had magical powers. In the fourth and fifth centuries AD St Augustine recommended its use in songs of joy to express the inexpressible. Some early Alleluias provide good examples of vocalise, many extending to a range of from 200 to 400 notes on one syllable. Coloratura cadenzas in opera, such as the Queen of the Night's extravagant aria in the second act of Mozart's _Die Zauberflöte_, are a form of secular vocalise. The solo soprano in _Le Rossignol et la rose_, by Saint-Saëns, sings a form of

RIGHT
This Alleluia is an example of vocalise. Note the four-line stave and archaic style of notation

A - l-le - lu ~ ia

ABOVE
Members of the chorus, with their vocal scores

vocalise. Debussy used women's voices in *Les Sirènes*, in a passage in which the creatures seem to loll languidly on pitching swell. Holst, who had an interest in the ancient mystical aspect of music, wrote for a wordless women's chorus in 'Neptune the Mystic,' from *The Planets*. Tenor and soprano are used singing wordlessly in Carl Nielsen's Third Symphony ('Expansiva'). Many composers have written passages extending the abilities of the singer as in earlier times they did that of the instruments. And some singers now have to imitate instruments. (It should be added that this is in fact an ancient practice; instrumental sounds have been vocalised as a means of teaching people how to play instruments. The method has long been used in Scotland for teaching the bagpipe, where it is called 'mouth music,' or *canntaireachd*.) The wheel has come full circle. Stockhausen includes hissing, shouting,

'Singing is so wholesome a pastime that it should be tried by all,' wrote one Victorian writer. The audience in this picture, 'Music in the Drawing Room' by Gavarini, seem to have their doubts

vocal clicks and speech sounds in his scores; George Crumb in his song cycle *Ancient Voices of Children* (1970) requires whispering and other special techniques. David Fanshaw, in his *African Mass*, has incorporated archaic forms of singing which he recorded in the Middle East, and which resemble the earliest forms of religious vocalise.

One of the most delightful examples of vocalise is Rossini's song 'The Two Cats,' a duet in which two sopranos start with some polite pedigree miaowing and end up spitting like alley cats.

Technique

There is a true story about the great Russian dramatic soprano Oda Slobodskaya, who could not pronounce 'th' in English. In describing vocal technique, she announced that 'You must always sing on the bread. Singing is all a question of breeding.' And indeed a combination of correct breathing and musical breeding is the foundation of a great voice: most readers will have noticed that many singers have strong, upright and rather ample figures. This is due to the fact that in order to make the maximum use of the lungs, the rib cage must be expanded, the diaphragm well supported and the breath drawn in generously without raising the shoulders and turning the face red. The belly itself balloons out when the lungs are filled and is drawn in when the air is exhaled. The body is a resonator, and the cavities of chest, throat, sinus and antrum (cavity of the upper jawbone) are all used to amplify the singing voice. (Many singers of a certain age have noticeably larger cheek bones and some have slight bulges over the eyebrows.) Various parts of the body resonators are used for different registers of the voice: chest for lower notes, middle for middle register and head for high notes. Just as a trombonist 'places' a note in his mind before playing it, so a singer, by some curious process of in-body thinking, places his notes, directing the sound from the boots upwards or direct from the top of the head. With a deep frown or scowl on the face, lower notes are produced than if the eyebrows are lifted; the latter expression of surprise, accompanied by a smile, raises the voice automatically.

The physiology of the mechanics of voice production is complex, and illustrations of the orifices and muscles involved are inclined to be gruesome. But there is one practical tip which is analogous to the act of singing: in the doctor's office when the patient is requested to say 'ah' while a spatula is inserted to hold down the tongue, the action of the muscles involved is the same as when the singer pronounces 'ah.' The epiglottis is raised, the tongue is naturally held forward behind the teeth, the throat is opened up, the doctor has a good look and the patient does not retch. The same effect is produced by yawning.

What is a beautiful voice? As has been suggested earlier, opinions vary and alter as regards ideal timbre. But whatever the timbre, it would seem from the earliest and still extant folk culture of, for example, the Balkans and ancient classical India, that mobility has been of constant importance since ancient times, through Monteverdi and onwards to Mozart and Rossini. This tradition produced generations of miraculously mobile voices, such as those of Tetrazzini, Adelina Patti and Jenny Lind (the Swedish Nightingale: the pagan idea of the supremacy and magic of the bird voice still rules) up to the incredible rippling of Joan Sutherland, Beverly Sills, Victoria de los Angeles, and others. But singers in our time have been said to revive a golden age, not create it. Great singing and writing for the voice in this spectacular manner dwindled at about the time sound recordings began. Then the countertenor, like the harpsichord earlier, became obsolete, as did the unearthly timbre of the male castrato (the last one of these was believed to be a Russian; his voice was recorded but the recording is impossible to obtain).

As the 19th century melted into the 20th, different styles of singing and different breeds of singers had evolved: on the one hand the great Wagnerian singers with phenomenal stamina, and on the other the smaller, Debussy-type voice, in, for example, his *Pelléas et Mélisande*. Then came Schoenberg's *sprechgesang* (speech singing) in *Pierrot Lunaire*, followed by Stockhausen and a host of *avant garde* compositions requiring vocal gymnastics no bird could accomplish. Thus today the instruments of the orchestra no longer imitate the voice, and the voice no longer imitates the bird. Simultaneously the revival of early European music has been accompanied by renewed interest in folk and classical cultures outside Europe. The countertenor has been restored and more ornamental mobility is demanded in all voices, as well as an open-throated timbre in which vibrato is used as ornamentation, rather than solely to add emotional power.

ABOVE
Leonardo da Vinci was an indefatigable investigator and designer of anything which caught his interest. This drawing of the human vocal equipment may have been done in connection with research into musical instruments

Voice repertoire

Mozart: Aria, *Der Hölle Rache Kocht in meinem Herzen* from *Die Zauberflöte*
Saint-Saëns: *Le Rossignol et la Rose*
Debussy: *Les Sirènes*
Holst: 'Neptune the Mystic' from *The Planets*
Nielson: Symphony No. 3 ('Expansiva')
Crumb: *Ancient Voices of Children*
Fanshaw: *African Mass*
Rossini: 'The Two Cats'
Debussy: *Pelléas et Mélisande*
Schoenberg: *Pierrot Lunaire*

Glossary

While not intended to be exhaustive, this list of definitions includes those considered to be most useful to readers of this book.

ACCIDENTAL see KEY.

ACOUSTIC
1. Anything to do with the sense of hearing.
2. The science of the behaviour and properties of sound.
3. The qualities of a resonator, such as a concert hall.

ARCO
Italian for 'bow'. Used in a score after a pizzicato passage indicating that the players are to resume using the bow. Also *coll'arco*, 'with the bow'.

AULOS
Greek name for double reed pipe.

BELL
Flared section at the end of the tubing of a wind instrument.

BORE
The inside diameter of a tube, e.g. a wind instrument.

BOUT
Curved shape on each side of a string instrument. Looks like a knee hole on the cello, but its purpose is acoustic.

CHALUMEAU
An early reed pipe, possibly ancestor of the clarinet. Still used to describe the low part of the clarinet's range.

CHROMATIC
Scale, chord, etc: including notes not part of the prevailing key (*q.v.*). Of an instrument: capable of being played in any key. See EQUAL TEMPERAMENT.

CLARINO
1. An early type of trumpet.
2. The highest part of the early trumpet's range.
3. Probably the word 'clarinet' comes from.

COMPASS
The range of notes of an instrument or a voice.

CONICAL
Like a cone, i.e. not cylindrical (*q.v.*).

CONTINUO
Accompanying, or filling in of harmonies, by means of playing from an outline of notes with figures beside them representing chords. Also called figured bass or thorough bass.

CROAK or CROW
The noise made by a double reed player when testing the reed for its pitch.

CROOK
1. The small tube carrying the reed of large instruments such as the bassoon.
2. Length of curved tubing added to an instrument to lengthen or shorten the tube, before the invention of valves. A length of straight tubing serving this purpose was called a shank.

CROSS FINGERING
Method of producing notes by means of different combinations of open and closed holes on a wind instrument. See FINGERING.

CUIVRÉ
A brassy sound produced on the horn by overblowing when the instrument is muted.

CYCLE
A single vibration of a sound, measured from a given point on the wave-form to the same point on the next wave-form. The frequency of a sound is the number of cycles per second (cps).

CYLINDRICAL
Of a wind instrument, or part of one: having a bore of continuous diameter, rather than graduated or conical.

DIATONIC
The diatonic scale is the scale of the white keys on the piano, starting from C. See also CHROMATIC, EQUAL TEMPERAMENT, KEY, MEAN TONE TUNING and MODE.

DIFFERENCE TONE
A clash of harmonics (*q.v.*) producing a sort of buzzing.

DIVISI
Instruction in a score to a group of instruments, e.g. cellos or basses, to divide into groups each playing different notes. Opposite of unison (*q.v.*).

DOUBLE STOP
On a bowed string instrument, playing two strings at once.

DOUBLING
1. Two instruments or groups playing the same tune or notes in unison, e.g. bassoons and basses, or violas and cellos.
2. Playing two instruments in the orchestra, e.g. oboe and English horn, flute and piccolo, or clarinet and saxophone (not at the same time!).

DOWN BEAT
Downward movement of conductor's arm indicating first beat of a bar.

DOWN BOW
Downward stroke of bow on violin or viola, from heel to tip.

DYNAMICS
The phenomenon of contrast between loud (forte) and soft (piano), or degrees of these. The dynamic range of an instrument is the range between the loudest and softest it can be played.

EMBOUCHURE
1. The shape of the lips and mouth of a wind player when playing. Often called just 'lip' in the case of brass players.
2. The blow hole of the flute.

EQUAL TEMPERAMENT
Tuning the notes of an adjustment so that chromatic scales and modulation from one key (*q.v.*) to another are possible. In doing this, certain notes, e.g. C sharp and D flat, are combined into one note which is acceptable if not perfectly accurate. The alternative would be an

impossible number of notes. Before equal temperament, a system of mean tone tuning (q.v.) made some keys perfect, others usable, and some intolerable.

EXTENDED RANGE
Addition to the working range of an instrument by means of the skill of the player, etc.

FIGURED BASS see CONTINUO.

FINGERING
The order and combination in which fingers are used to produce notes. There may be many different ways to produce a given note; the best way is partly a matter of opinion and depends on circumstances such as necessary agility in a rapid passage.

FIRST DESK
The leading member of a section in an orchestra. Also called principal.

FLUTTER TONGUING
The rolling of an R behind the teeth when playing a wind instrument.

FOOT
4 foot, 8 foot, 16 foot, 32 foot. These terms refer to the length of the longest (and lowest sounding) pipe in a rank (or row) of pipes in an organ. With 8 foot for the longest pipe the range of notes sounds at the same pitch as the piano; half the length sounds an octave above and twice the length an octave below. This convention of naming pitches is also used for the sets of strings in a harpsichord.

FOOT JOINT
Bottom section of flute.

FORK FINGERING see CROSS FINGERING.

FORMANT
The combination of a tone plus its overtones, or the first partial and the upper partials, which give an instrument or a voice its characteristic sound, or timbre. Overtones, partials and harmonics are not all the same thing; a partial might not be harmonic in character. Similarly, timbre and formant are not quite the same thing. A plastic and a wooden bassoon will differ in the quality of their respective timbre, but they will both be recognized as bassoons because of the characteristic formant, in the same way we recognize a friend's voice even on a bad telephone line.

FREQUENCY see CYCLE.

FUNDAMENTAL
The note produced by a pipe or string sounding its whole length, and therefore its lowest note.

GARLAND
The flared part of the bell (q.v.) of a brass instrument, where the maker's name is usually engraved.

GLISSANDO
The playing of a series of adjacent notes. On the piano or the harp, the rippling effect is the consequence of a series of distinct notes without emphasis on any single note; a glissando on a single string of a bowed instrument, or (with more skill required in coordinating fingers and embouchure) on a wind instrument, the effect is a sliding series of an infinite number of pitches.

HAND HORN
The pre-valve horn, with which the hand in the bell or a crook (q.v.) was used to alter the pitch. Also called natural horn.

HARMONIC
A vibrating string or column of air produces a fundamental (q.v.), but it also vibrates in smaller equal parts, producing harmonics.

HEAD JOINT
Top section of the flute, including the embouchure (q.v.).

HITCH PIN
A type of pin in the tail end of a piano or a harpsichord, around which the string is held fast.

INTONATION
The player's pitch; hence 'good' or 'bad' intonation means in or out of tune.

JACK
Thin, oblong strip of wood in a harpsichord which holds the quill (q.v.). When a key is depressed the jack leaps up and the quill plucks a string; the quill is inserted in a small hinged device which, when it falls back by gravitational force, drops clear of the string.

KEY
A somewhat mysterious subject, difficult to explain briefly. There are twelve semitones to an octave. Each of these can be used as the basis (keynote or tonic) for two different progressions of notes: major (generally suitable for jolly music) or minor (for sad music). In theory it should not make any difference whether a piece of music is in C major or A major, but since the adoption of equal temperament (q.v.) in order to build chromatic (q.v.) instruments, the octave is not divided into twelve perfectly equal parts. The system of tuning is a compromise, and the keys sound different, with the differences becoming more pronounced in the extreme registers of the instruments.

Unlike a mode (q.v.), however, a key is not established by the progression of notes alone, but by the addition of other notes in the harmonic series, i.e. the fifth, fourth and third. Any note not belonging to the original progression is called an accidental. Key changes, or modulations (q.v.), in a piece of music are often achieved by means of accidentals, but those achieved without any preparation at all (from the point of view of the listener) are the most thrilling or daring. This foundation of harmonic progression has gradually been weakened, first of all by chromaticism (a sort of gliding along from semitone to semitone), practised by composers such as Wagner, Bruckner and Mahler, and then by atonal music, which abandons the security of the home key altogether. Schoenberg (1874–1951) was the first to write atonal or twelve-tone music, and it is interesting to note that Vaughan Williams (1872–1958), during the same period, was introducing a form of modal music based on his admiration of the English folk song.

LEADER
The first violinist. In the USA he is called the concert master, and he has many duties as leader of the orchestra and assistant to the conductor, as well as principal (q.v.) of the violin section.

LEDGER LINES
Short lines drawn above or below the stave, for notes

which are too high or low to be accommodated on the stave. Sometimes spelled 'leger'.

LEGATO
Passage to be played with smooth transitions between the notes; opposite of staccato.

LIP
Used to describe the embouchure (q.v.) of the brass player.

MEAN TONE TUNING
Precursor of equal temperament (q.v.) tuning, common until about 1750 and still used in Britain for church organs until well into the 19th century. In mean tone tuning some keys (q.v.) sounded more pleasing than others, and were more useful, while the relative tuning of others made certain modulations (q.v.) between keys impossible.

MODES
Progressions of notes in which the different spacing between them (tones and semitones) occur in different orders. The first modes were established by Pythagoras in ancient Greece. These eventually came under the scrutiny of various church fathers, especially St Ambrose and St Gregory, until the number of permutations was increased to twelve, producing what were called ecclesiastical modes; these are still used for Gregorian plainsong. In secular music the number of modes diminished until two progressions survived: the major and minor modes, now called keys (q.v.).

MODULATION
Change from one key to another within a composition.

MUTE
A device which attenuates overtones, thus quietening and altering the sound of a musical instrument.

NATURAL HORN see HAND HORN.

OBBLIGATO
Obligatory; not to be omitted. The opposite would be ad libitum: at pleasure, or as you like.

OCTAVE
An interval of eight notes (or twelve semitones).

OPEN NOTE
Note produced from a pipe with all the keys open.

OPEN STRING
An unstopped string, which therefore produces its fundamental (q.v.)

OVERBLOW
An increase of wind pressure which produces a series of harmonics (q.v.).

PARABOLIC
A parabola is a curve, or curved shape, such that anything aimed at it from its focal point will be reflected in a controlled way. Thus the reflecting surface in an automobile headlamp is a parabola, so that the light travels out of the lamp in a straight line; and the parabola has been found to be the most efficient shape for the head joint of a flute.

PEDAL NOTE
Bottom note, produced on the trombone (for example) when the slide is fully extended.

PIROUETTE
On a shawm or a folk oboe, the disc below the staple

against which the player presses his mouth.

PITCH
The level of a note in the sound spectrum. Intervals are relative, but pitch is absolute: e.g. A is internationally agreed to be 440 cps. See CYCLE.

POLYPHONIC
Word of Greek origin meaning 'many voices'. The basis of composition in pre-classical music; thus instrumentation rather than orchestration was important; any instruments could be used as long as the voices remained distinct, rather than chosen by the composer himself for their individual tone colour, or timbre (q.v.).

PRINCIPAL see FIRST DESK.

QUILL
Part of the flight feather of a large bird, used to pluck the string in a harpsichord. See JACK.

REGISTER
Division of the compass (q.v.) of an instrument for convenience; e.g. high, medium, low.

RESONATOR
Any vessel of any size or material which conducts or amplifies a sound: the body of an instrument, the concert platform and the conductor's podium, the hall itself.

SCORDATURA
Italian meaning 'out of tuning'. Alternative or special tuning of stringed instrument in order to obtain temporarily wider compass (q.v.), to facilitate a difficult passage or to make possible unusual double stops (q.v.).

SCORE
Full score or orchestral score shows all the music on separate staves for each part; the 'parts' of a score show the separate parts for each instrument or group; the piano score or reduction is self describing: this was particularly common before the invention of the gramophone, so that symphonies etc. could be played at home on the piano; the vocal score shows all the voice parts of an opera or oratorio, with the orchestral part reduced: miniature or pocket scores are for students or music lovers to study or follow.

SLIDE
1. Part of a trombone pushed and pulled by the player. 2. Piece of adjustable tubing on brass instrument for tuning. 3. Part of tube which fits into socket on another part (of wind instrument which can be dismantled).

SPEAK, TO SPEAK
To produce a note (of an instrument). Thus low-pitched instruments such as the bass or the bassoon are slower to 'speak' because it takes more power to overcome the inertia of a longer or thicker string or column of air.

STACCATO
Italian 'detached', i.e. separate and distinct notes. Opposite of legato (q.v.).

STAPLE
Section of an instrument in which a reed is mounted and which is fitted into the body.

STAVE
Set of five lines on which music is written, to which ledger lines (q.v.) are added if necessary. Early music, such as Gregorian chants, had only four-line staves.

TEMPERING see *EQUAL TEMPERAMENT*.

TEMPO

Italian 'speed'. The time signature in a score gives the number of beats in a measure, but the tempo is up to the conductor. A score (*q.v.*) might include many instructions about tempo, for example *a tempo*, which means 'resume regular speed' after an *accelerando*.

THOROUGH BASS See *CONTINUO*.

TIBIA

Roman name for double reed pipe.

TIMBRE

Quality of sound of an instrument, which depends upon the number of harmonics in relation to the fundamental. See also *FORMANT*.

TRANSCRIBE

To re-arrange a piece for an instrument or group of instruments other than that for which it was written. Applied both to reductions (as Liszt's piano transcriptions of Beethoven's symphonies) or orchestrations (such as Ravel's orchestration of Mussorgsky's *Pictures at an Exhibition*). Another example would be Beethoven's own arrangement of his Violin Concerto for piano and orchestra, which he did because a publisher offered him money for it.

TRANSIENT

Literally, 'brief'. Refers to the precise moment when a note is produced and when the maximum number of harmonics is present in the sound, giving the main clue to the identity of the instrument producing it. Could be called 'starting sound'.

TRANSPOSE

To write or play a piece of music to a higher or a lower key. Usually done for the convenience of a singer. Also, transposing instrument: one which is not written for at its natural pitch, but which produces the effect of that pitch.

TUTTI

Italian 'all together'.

UNISON

A group of players all to play the same notes or tune; opposite of 'divisi' (*q.v.*).

UPBEAT

Upward movement of conductor's arm to indicate second beat in a bar.

UPBOW

Violin or viola bow drawn from tip to heel.

VALVE

Mechanical device which allows access of breath to additional tubing in a brass instrument, thus changing its pitch. There are two types: piston valves (as on the trumpet) and rotary valves (used on many modern trombones). Some instruments, such as the French horn, can be had with either. The musical instrument trade makes a distinction between *valves* (pistons) and *rotors* (rotary valves).

VIBRATO

The 'trembling' of a note by means of continuous fluctuation of pitch. Sometimes confused with tremolo, which is the rapid repetition of a note, or the rapid alternation of two notes.

VOICE, TO VOICE

To make refinements to the sound of an instrument. Particularly used in reference to adjusting pitch and timbre (*q.v.*) of organ pipes, and adjusting felt on hammers in a piano.

VOX HUMANA

Latin 'human voice'. 1. A stop on the organ. 2. The high register (*q.v.*) of the bassoon.

WREST PIN

Adjustable screw used for tuning the strings in a piano or a harpsichord. Also called tuning pin.

WREST PLANK

Plank into which are screwed the wrest pins (*q.v.*) in a piano or a harpsichord.

Bibliography

This is a brief and select bibliography, to supplement such obvious scholarly sources as the quarterly *Early Music*, published by Oxford University Press, the publications of the Horniman Museum, *Eighteenth Century Musical Instruments: France and Britain* and *Wind Instruments of European Art Music*, Sir George Grove's *Dictionary of Music and Musicians*, published by MacMillan (1899 ed.), and *Larousse de la Musique* (1957).

BAINES, Anthony *European Musical Instruments* Batsford, 1966
  (Ed) *Musical Instruments Through the Ages* Pelican, 1961
BATE, Philip *The Oboe* Benn, 1975
  The Trumpet and the Trombone Benn, 1978
BERLIOZ, Hector *Instrumentation* Novello, 1882
BEVAN, Clifford *The Tuba Family* Faber, 1978
BONANNI, Filippo *The Showcase of Musical Instruments* Dover, 1964
BOULT, Sir Adrian *Thoughts on Conducting* Phoenix, 1963
CAMDEN, Archie *Bassoon Technique* Oxford, 1962
CANDÉ, Roland de *Dictionnaire de Musique* Editions du Sevil, 1961
FITZGIBBON, H. Macaulay *The Flute* Walter Scott, 1914
HAWKINS, Sir John *A General History of the Science and Practice of Music* Dover, 1963
HELMHOLZ, Hermann L.F. *On Sensations of Tone* Dover, 1954
LANG, Paul Henry *Music in Western Civilization* Norton, 1941
LANGWILL, Lyndesay G. *The Bassoon and Contrabassoon* Benn, 1975

MARCUSE, Sibyl *Musical Instruments: a Comprehensive Dictionary* Country Life, 1964
  A Survey of Musical Instruments David and Charles, 1975
MORLEY–PEGGE, R. *The French Horn* Benn, 1973
MUNROW, David *Instruments of the Middle Ages and Renaissance* Oxford, 1976
NELSON, Sheila M. *The Violin and Viola* Benn, 1972
PANUM, Hortense *Stringed Instruments of the Middle Ages* W. Reeves, 1971
PISTON, Walter *Orchestration* Gollancz, 1955
QUANTZ J.J. *On Playing the Flute* Dover, 1966
READ, Gardner *Thesaurus of Orchestral Devices* Pitman, 1953
RENDALL, F. Geoffrey *The Clarinet* Benn, 1971
RENSCH, Roslyn *The Harp* Duckworth, 1969
RIMMER, Joan *The Irish Harp* The Government of Ireland, 1969
  Ancient Musical Instruments of Western Asia British Museum, 1969
RIMSKY–KORSAKOV, Nicolas *Principes d'Orchestration* Edition Russe de Musique, 1921
ROCKSTRO, R.S. *The Flute* Rudall Carte and Co., 1928
SACHS, Kurt *The History of Musical Instruments* Dent, 1968
SCHOLES, Percy *The Oxford Companion to Music* Oxford 1975
WELCH, Christopher *History of the Boehm Flute* Rudall Carte and Co., 1892
WESTON, Pamela *The Clarinet Teacher's Companion* Hale, 1976
WOOD, Alexander *The Physics of Music* Methuen, 1944

Picture acknowledgements

Permission to reproduce photographs has kindly been granted by the following:

Black-and-White
From the author's collection: 25; Bayerische Staatsbibliothek, Munich: 18; BBC Hulton Picture Library: 13, 96 (right), 114, 115, 117, 122, 126, 147, 157, 168; Biblioteca Nazionale, Naples: 102 (above); Boosey and Hawkes Ltd: 111; British Library: 41; British Museum: 2; Gene Carr: 158 (left); Chicago Symphony Orchestra: 10 (above), 38, 42, 62, 92, 148; Cleveland Orchestra: 29; Crown copyright, Victoria and Albert Museum: 68; Gerald Drucker: 101, 110, 158 (right); Courtesy of Mark Gardner: 56; Anthony Haas: 50, 104, 107, 143, 154; Horniman Museum: 72; London Philharmonic Orchestra: 77; Mansell Collection: 17, 36, 60, 80, 86, 90, 96 (left), 102 (below), 103, 121, 133, 134, 138, 139, 166; Metro-Goldwyn-Mayer Inc: 83; Musée des Beaux Arts, Budapest: 49; Musée Instrumentale du Conservatoire National de Musique, Paris: 66; Museum für Kunst und Gewerbe, Hamburg: 10 (below); National Portrait Gallery, London: 153; National Trust for Scotland: 8–9; Nationalmuseet, Copenhagen: 78; Neidersachsische Staats und Universisatsbibliothek, Göttingen: 9; Philharmonia Orchestra: 94, 161; Royal Library, Windsor Castle, reproduced by Gracious Permission of Her Majesty the Queen: 167; Staatliche Kunstsammlungen, Dresden: 130; Brian Tufano: 32, 59; Western Orchestral Society Ltd: 74, 82.

Colour
A.F. Kersting: 141; Premier Drum Company Ltd: 106, 123, 124. The following were specially photographed for this book: A.C. Cooper Ltd: 33, 142, 159, 160; Dudley Reed: 34, 51, 52, 69, 70, 87, 88, 105.
The publishers wish to thank the following for their assistance in lending instruments for the special photography: Rudall Carte Ltd (flutes); Charles Foote Ltd (double bass); W.E. Hill and Sons (violin and viola); Heather Jones (cello); Bill Lewington Ltd (all brass and remaining woodwind); Salvi Harpmakers Ltd (harp).

Permission to reproduce excerpts from music in copyright has kindly been granted by the following: Boosey and Hawkes Music Publishers Ltd, London (Mussorgsky's *Pictures at an Exhibition* orchestrated by Ravel); Chappell Music Ltd *(Rhapsody in Blue* Music by George Gershwin © 1924 Harms Inc. [Warner Bros.]); Durand et Cie, Paris /U.M.P. (Ravel's *Boléro*); Schott and Company Ltd London (Tippett's *Second Symphony*).

Index

Numbers in italics refer to
illustrations
Numbers in bold refer to
chapters on individual
instruments

A

Academy of St Martin-in-the-Fields,
14
Amati family, violin makers, 138,
143, 146, 151, 161
Angeles, Victoria de los, 167
Appian Way columbarium, 36
Armstrong, Louis (1900–71), 83, 83
Astor flute, 33
aulos, 35, 41

B

Bach, C.P.E. (1714–88), 119, 121
figured bass, 23, 119
Bach, J.S. (1685–1750), 12, 14, 26,
28, 48, 79, 81, 121
B Minor Mass, 119
Brandenburg concerti, 82, 140
Christmas Oratorio, 44
48 Preludes and Fugues, 16, 117
Suite in B minor, 39
Bach, J.C. (1735–82), 122
'Bach trumpet', 79, 81
Baffo, Giovanni, harpsichord by, 118
bagpipe, 13, 165
Balakirev, Mily, 164
barrel organs, 114
Bartók, Béla (1881–1945), 104, 155
Concerto for Orchestra, 39, 63
Dance Suite, 127
Divertimento for String Orchestra,
145
Music for Strings, Percussion and
Celesta, 108, 145
Viola Concerto, 149
bass drum (Turkish drum), 109, 109
basset-clarinet, 20
bassoon, 13, 58–63, 69
double or contra-, 59, 63
BBC Symphony Orchestra, 59, 135
Beecham, Sir Thomas, 26
Beethoven, Ludwig van (1770–1827),
13, 24, 26, 27, 28, 45, 63, 93,
102, 115, 125, 126, 146, 154,
157
Egmont overture, 20, 79
Fifth Piano Concerto, 155
Fifth Symphony, 29, 93, 145, 149,
161
First Piano Concerto, 14, 15

First Symphony, 145
Fourth Piano Concerto, 127, 155
Funeral Equali, 93
Leonora No. 3 overture, 38, 82
Ninth Symphony ('Choral'), 14,
27, 104, 109, 126
Sextet for String Quartet and Two
Horns, 74
Sixth Symphony ('Pastoral'), 39,
44, 45, 161
Third Symphony ('Eroica'), 79
Violin Concerto, 103, 104
beme, 76
Berio, Luciano (b. 1925), *Sequenza*,
135
Berlioz, Hector (1803–69), 17, 18, 27,
28, 45, 80–81, 86, 91, 93, 108,
111, 115, 146, 157, 164
Damnation of Faust, 134
Harold in Italy, 149
Requiem, 24, 104
Symphonie fantastique, 44
Treatise on Instrumentation, 38, 77,
79
The Trojans, 74
Biber, Heinrich von, 144
Bizet, Georges (1838–75), 57, 164
Blanc, Hubert de, 154–5
Blanton, Jimmy, 158
Bliss, Arthur (b. 1891):
Lie Strewn the White Flocks, 39
'Pastoral', 104
Boehm, Theobald (1793–1881), 36–7
Bonanni, Filippo, 61
Borodin, Alexander, 164
Bottesini, Giovanni (1821–89), 157
Boulez, Pierre, 135
Boult, Sir Adrian, 28, 29
Bournemouth Sinfonietta, 74, 82
Brahms, Johannes (1833–97), 15, 97,
126
Clarinet Quintet, 53
Second Piano Concerto, 75, 75,
127, 155
Second Symphony, 97
Brinsmead, John, piano by, 122
Britten, Benjamin (1913–1976):
Sinfonia da Requiem, 57
*Young Person's Guide to the
Orchestra*, 39
Broadwood pianos, 121, 122
Bruckner, Anton (1824–96), 97
bugle horns, 94
Bülow, Hans von (1830–94), 27–8

C

Caballé, Montserrat, 167
Cahusac, instrument maker, 43
Cambert, Robert (1628–77), 62

Pomone, 44, 62
carnyx (Celtic trumpet), 78, 79
castanets, 110, 110
castrato, 167
celesta, 107–8
Cerveny, instrument makers, 97
Challen piano, 126
Chaucer, Geoffrey, 131
cello, 150–55, 160
Chicago Symphony Orchestra, 10,
38, 42, 62, 92, 148
Chickering, Jonas, piano maker, 121,
122
chimes, or tubular bells, 108, 124
Chodowiecki, Daniel, 13, 117
Chopin, Frédéric (1810–49), 126
cittern, 13
clarinet, 20, 29, 46–53, 55
bass, 48, 48, 49, 51
contrabass, 40
clarioun, 76
Clarke, Jeremiah (c. 1670–1707),
Trumpet Voluntary, 82
clavichord, 13
Clementi, Muzio (1752–1832), 125,
126
Cleveland Symphony Orchestra, 29
Collegium Musicum, Jena, 10
coloratura cadenzas, 164
compasses of instruments, 8, 19–20
Concanen, Alfred, 25
concert-master *see* leader of the
orchestra
conductor, conducting, 24–9
contrabassoon, 59, 63
Copland, Aaron (b. 1900), 127
First Symphony, 149
Rodeo, 145, 161
El Salón México, 50
Symphony for Organ and
Orchestra, 115
Viola Concerto, 149
cor anglais (English horn), 16, 34, 45
cor de chasse, 68, 73
Corelli, Arcangelo (1653–1713), 140
Corkhill, David, 110
cornett, 13, 60
countertenor, 167
Couperin, François (1668–1733), 117
L'Art de Toucher le Clavecin, 116
Cousineau, harp maker, 133
Covent Garden promenade concert,
25
cowbells, 14
Crathes Castle, Scotland, 8–9
Cremonese School of violin makers,
138, 140, 146
Crétien, R., hunting horn by, 66
Cristofori, B., piano maker, 120, 121
crotales, 110
Crumb, George, *Ancient Voices of
Children*, 166

shawm, *13*, 42, *60*
Shore, Bernard, 146
Shostakovitch, Dmitri (b. 1906), 97,
    111, 127
    Second Piano Concerto, 127
Sibelius, Jean (1865–1957), 104, 155
    First Symphony, 135
    The Swan of Tuonela, 135
side drum *see* snare drum
Silberman, Gottfried, piano maker,
    121
Sills, Beverly, 167
Slobodskaya, Oda, 166
Smith, Andrew, timpanist, *101*
snare drum, *108*, **108–9**
Solti, Sir George, *10*, *148*
son cuivré, 73
Sousaphone, 96
speech singing, Schoenberg's, 167
Spohr, Louis (1784–1859), 140
Stamitz, Karl (1746–1801), 146, 147
Stanesby, instrument maker, 43
Steimer, Jacob, *89*
Stimmer, Tobias (1539–84), *80*
Stockhausen, Karlheinz (b. 1928),
    165–6, 167
Stokowski, Leopold, 21, 28
Stölzel, Heinrich, 71
Stradivari, Antonio, violin maker,
    140
Strauss, Richard (1864–1949), 8, 14,
    24, 27, 75, 104, 115, 161
    Alpine Symphony, 93
    Sinfonia Domestica, 44, 57
Stravinsky, Igor (1882–1971), 27, 97,
    161
    Firebird, 155
    Petrushka, 127
    Rite of Spring, 63

T

tamborine, *13*, **109**
tam-tams, **111**
Tartini, Giuseppe (1693–1770), 140
Taylor, Henry, timpanist, 104
Tchaikovsky, Peter (1840–93), 39,
    164
    1812 Overture, 108
    Fifth Symphony, 63, 75
    First Piano Concerto, 127
    Nutcracker, 50, 107, 108, 135

tenor or military drum, 109
Tertis, Lionel, viola player, 146, 147,
    147
Tetrazzini, 167
Thibouville-Lamy violins, 143
thunder machine, 14
tibia, 35
timbre, 15–16, 17, 19
timpani (kettle drums), *14*, **100–106**,
    106
    nakers, 100, 102, *102*
    pedal drums, *101*, 103, 104, *104*
Tippett, Sir Michael (b. 1905), 127
    Concerto for Orchestra, 127
    Third Symphony, 14, 111, 127
Toscanini, Arturo, 26, *29*
Tourte, François (1747–1835), 140
training of instrumentalists, 22–4
transient, 16
triangle, *13*, 110, **111**, *111*
Triébert, Frédéric, 43
trombone, 20, **84–93**
    bass, *13*, 91
    contrabass, 91
    sackbut, 85–6, *86*, 89, *89*
    slide, 89–91, *91*
    valve, 89, *90*
trumpet, *13*, **76–83**, *87*
    'Bach', 79, 81
    principals and clarino players,
      79–80, 81, 82
    valve, *80*, 80–81
tuba, 20, **94–7**, *105*
tubular bells, **108**, *124*
Turkish drum, 109
Turkish music, 102, 104, 109

U

Ueno Academy Orchestra, Japan, 9

V

Vaughan Williams, Ralph
    (1872–1958):
    Job ballet, 57
    Tuba Concerto, 97
Verdi, Giuseppe (1813–1901), 27
viola (da braccio), 140, **146–9**, *159*
viola da gamba, *9*, *18*, *117*, 140, 150,
    153, *153*

violin(s), *117*, **136–45**, *159*
    bow, 140, 144
violoncello *see* cello
viols, *13*, 140
Vivaldi, Antonio (1676–1741), 63
vocalise (wordless singing), 164–6
the voice, 12, **164–7**

W

Wagner, Richard (1813–83), 8, 21,
    27, 80–81, 82–3, 91, 93, 97, 164
    Flying Dutchman, 75
    Gotterdämmerung, 14
    Die Meistersinger, 97
    Rienzi Overture, 83
    Der Ring des Nibelungen, 97, 134
    Tristan and Isolde, 28, 75
Wagner, Tuben, 97, *97*
Walton, William (b. 1902), Viola
    Concerto, 149
wayghtes or waits, 41
Weber, Carl Maria von (1786–1826),
    27, 28, 45, 111, 164
    Bassoon Concerto, 63
    Clarinet Concerto, 53
    Der Freischütz Overture, 53, 93
    Oberon overture, 74
Webster, Ben, 57
Welsh harp, 132
Westminster Abbey organ, *115*
Wieprecht, Wilhelm, 96

X

xylophone, *13*, *107*, 108

Y

Young, Lester, 57

Z

Zumpe, Johannes, piano maker, 122